Tony Evans - April 08

see also:-

"Spheres of Flying: the Politics of International
aviation" International Organisation 35:2
1980

International
Politics of ...

Chinese Foreign ...

Department ... and Asia
University ...

# International Aviation and the Politics of Regime Change

Christer Jönsson

Department of Political Science
University of Lund, Sweden

Frances Pinter (Publishers), London

First published in Great Britain in 1987 by
Frances Pinter (Publishers) Limited
25 Floral Street, London WC2E 9DS

**British Library Cataloguing in Publication Data**

Jönsson, Christer
    International aviation and the politics
    of regime change.
    1. Aeronautics, Commercial—Political
    aspects—History
    I. Title
    387.7′4  HE9777

    ISBN 0-86187-695-4

Typeset by MCL Computerset Ltd, Ely, Cambs, England.
Printed by Biddles of Guildford Ltd.

# Contents

# Acknowledgements

The subject area of international aviation makes for suggestive imagery and associations. My colleagues and friends have alternately commented on my high-flying plans, wondered whether I was working on a pilot study, and characterized my results as 'a lot of hot air.' In the same vein, I want to extend my thanks to all those who have assisted my project from takeoff to landing, through clear skies as well as turbulence.

The idea of studying the political aspects of international air transport was originally suggested to me by Gordon Bayless, Jr., an old friend and former IATA official, who has also contributed helpful comments on earlier drafts. I am indebted to numerous officials of IATA, ICAO, and United States and Swedish aviation authorities who have given generously of their time in interviews. Special thanks are due to Knut Hammarskjöld, Geoffrey Lipman and Peter Harbison for their support and encouragement throughout the project.

This study is part of a larger project labelled 'States and International Organizations.' The financial support from the Bank of Sweden Tercentenary Foundation and the invaluable intellectual contributions of my co-pilots in the project, Professor Lars-Göran Stenelo and Research Assistants Staffan Bolin and Ragnhild Ek, are gratefully acknowledged. Stefan Persson has been of great help in computerizing my flight.

I made several test flights before setting out on this long-haul journey. Preliminary research reports have been presented at international conferences, often with financial support from the Nordic Cooperation Committee for International Politics. I have integrated into some of the chapters, in revised form, parts of two articles published in *International Organization* (Jönsson, 1981) and *International Studies Quarterly* (Jönsson, 1986a). I appreciate the publishers' permission to do this.

Any flight is dependent on good traffic control in order to keep on course. The Department of Political Science at the University of Lund has been my ground control. Interaction with my colleagues has insured me against going astray. I especially want to thank Lennart Lundquist and Björn Beckman for guiding me through the new and unfamiliar terrain of organization theory.

It is customary to depict one's family as the service and maintenance crew: indispensable for a successful flight but not part of the adventure. That is only partially true of my wife Evy and my children Lena and Linus. Their support and patience have indeed been indispensable, but they have taken an active part in the adventure. For this, and many other things, I owe them an immeasurable debt of gratitude.

# Introduction

This book has been written with a dual audience in mind. To the specialist in international aviation it offers a somewhat novel perspective on familiar events as well as certain new insights into lesser-known political processes in the issue-area. To students of international politics it purports to make a contribution to the ongoing debate concerning 'complex interdependence' and the study of 'international regimes' by providing a detailed illustration of, and further developing, theories of regime creation and change.

## Complex interdependence and international regimes

The past decade has witnessed heated discussions among international relations scholars about the changing international system. Some argue that global changes have been so profound as to warrant a 'paradigm shift;' others have wondered whether it is really the world that has been transformed or the perceptions and attention of scholars that have changed to include new areas of international relations previously overlooked.

The observed global changes — such as the paradoxes of military strength in the nuclear age, the rapid increase in transaction flows, the emergence of new international actors besides states, the blurring of the borderline between national societies and their international environment, and the dissemination of 'spaceship earth' ideas — have been subsumed under the summary concept 'interdependence.'

Robert Keohane and Joseph Nye, in a landmark study (1977), outline the 'ideal type' of *complex interdependence* which they contrast with the traditional 'realist' ideal type of the international system. Whereas the 'realists' emphasize the role of sovereign states relying on military force in a basically anarchic international system, the main characteristics of complex interdependence are these:

(1) Multiple channels connect national societies. These channels include interstate, transgovernmental, and transnational relations. States do not necessarily act coherently as units; individual government departments and agencies maintain contacts with their counterparts in other states. This is referred to as transgovernmental relations. Transnational relations are those in which states or state agencies are not the interacting units.

(2) There is no hierarchy among issues on the international agenda, headed by questions of military security, as the realist perspective would assume. Instead, agenda setting and efforts to link issues become important parts of international relations.

(3) Military force plays a minor role in settling international issues. Employing force against a state with which one has a variety of relationships is likely to rupture mutually profitable relations. And military force is irrelevant to the solution of a host of pressing international problems (for instance: how do you solve the world's debt crisis by military means?).

The summary concept of interdependence 'has a number of misleading implicit connotations, the most common among these being cooperation and symmetry' (Reynolds & McKinlay, 1979: 160). This is recognized not only by its critics but also by adherents of the interdependence school, who lament that 'rhetorical uses of "interdependence" frequently carry highly positive and egalitarian overtones,' which 'have affected the way analysts have used the term, sometimes with detrimental effects on conceptual clarity' (Keohane & Nye, 1975: 367). Repudiating such misleading connotations, Keohane and Nye (1977: 8) repeatedly stress that under interdependence 'conflict will take new forms, and may even increase,' and Edward Morse (1976: 149–50) even claims that 'instead of laying the basis for a new era of international harmony, interdependence seems to magnify international tensions and to stress national differences.'

In short, realism and the interdependence school alike focus on the interplay of conflict and cooperation in the international system, albeit from different perspectives.

Whereas the attention of realist scholars has concentrated on security issues, students of interdependence have brought international political economy — 'the reciprocal and dynamic interaction in international relations of the pursuit of wealth and the pursuit of power' (Gilpin, 1975: 43) — back into focus. The interaction of politics and economics has been an old theme in the study of international relations, from seventeenth-century mercantilists to present-day Marxists. Yet in our century politics and economics have largely been divorced from each other in Western academic studies, as a result of the predominance of liberalist thought and the specialization of modern academe (cf. Spero, 1977: 1–2). The interdependence school entails the rediscovery of international political economy.

The debate between 'realists' and proponents of the 'complex interdependence' model has raised the question of whether it is at all meaningful to speak of a *single* international system. A more appropriate conceptualization might be in terms of 'multiple issue-based systems,' with each system featuring a unique cast of actors dealing with a discrete set of issues, yet with linkages between systems either because of overlap among participant actors or because of the interdependence of the issues upon which they focus (Lampert *et al.*, 1978). In lieu of the classic 'billiard-ball' model in which international interaction is seen to be governed by the relative size and power of solid, impermeable units, this perspective evokes the imagery of 'a mass of cobwebs superimposed on one another, strands converging at some points more than others, and being concentrated between some points more than between others' (Burton, 1972: 43).

The most appropriate research strategy would then seem to be to analyze each issue-based 'cobweb' separately in order, at a later stage, to compare notes and look for patterns across issue-areas. Keohane and Nye's (1977) study took a significant step in that direction. At the same time, it has spurred interest among international relations scholars in focussing on the creation and evolution of cooperative arrangements, or 'regimes,' in their studies of politico-economic issue-areas.

## Why study international aviation?

International civil aviation appears to be a pertinent yet largely overlooked issue-area to study from this vantage point. First, the development of international air transport has actively contributed to the observed trend toward interdependence in contemporary world affairs by facilitating the rapid flow of goods and people across national boundaries. International civil aviation is also an economic activity of considerable magnitude, representing today, together with tourism, the largest single world trade item after petroleum. More important yet, the aviation issue-area displays a rare combination of security aspects generally attributed to the traditional 'anarchy' or 'realist' models and economic aspects associated with the new interdependence models.

Students of international regimes have sometimes been accused of selecting issue-areas in such a way that their hypotheses are 'doomed to success.' Realists claim that, by focussing on 'low politics' issue-areas, regime studies find trends toward interdependence which do not pertain to the 'high politics' of security issues. Put differently, the purported study of the international political economy is criticized for placing more emphasis on the 'pursuit of wealth' than on the 'pursuit of power.'

International aviation, however, differs from most business involving services or commodities by directly engaging the national security interests, the sovereignty, and the prestige of almost all countries of the world.

International aviation is thus not just another problem in a changing economic system, though it is that; international civil aviation is a serious problem in international relations, affecting the way governments view one another, the way individual citizens view their own and foreign countries, and in a variety of direct and indirect connections the security arrangements by which we live. (Lowenfeld, 1975: 36.)

In a recent popular history of the international airlines, Anthony Sampson (1985: 24) puts it thus:

Airlines and politics have collided with each other from the beginning. The airlines, as they changed the shape of the world, were also locked into the ambitions of nations. They provide a kind of visual projection of changes on earth — the shifting political balances of power and wealth, the swings of economic beliefs, the technological developments coming up against political deadlocks and reactions.

From the outset of air communications, civil and military aviation have been interconnected. As a matter of fact, this interconnection was foreseen long before man had the ability to fly. Already by the seventeenth century, the Jesuit priest Francesco de Lana-Terzi was writing in vivid detail about future military uses of aircraft, including bombing, troop transports and invasion, and concluded that 'God would not suffer such an invention to take effect, by reason of the disturbance it would cause to civil government of men' (Emme, 1959: 3; Gibbs-Smith, 1967: 3).

In 1759 Samuel Johnson stated the problem in *The History of Rasselas, Prince of Abyssinia* through one of the book's characters, who was building wings designed to enable man to fly: 'If all men were virtuous . . . I should with great alacrity teach them all to fly. But what would be the security of the good, if the bad could at pleasure invade them from the sky?' (quoted in Cooper, 1947: 9). Benjamin Franklin, who witnessed the first balloon flights near Paris in 1783, wrote to a friend about this 'discovery of great importance': 'Convincing Sovereigns of the Folly of wars may perhaps be one Effect of it, since it will be impracticable for the most potent of them to guard his Dominions' (quoted in Cooper, 1947: 11).

Sir George Cayley, who invented the concept of a powered airplane in 1799, foresaw in 1809 that 'a new era in society will commence from the moment that aerial navigation is familiarly realised'; his vision emphasized the commercial potentials of flight, predicting that 'we shall be able to transport ourselves and families, and their goods and chattels, more securely by air than by water' (Gibbs-Smith, 1967: 12).

Lord Tennyson's eloquent but less sanguine prophecy in *Locksley Hall*, published in 1842, pointed to the inextricable linkages between the civil and military aviation:

For I dipt into the future,
    far as human eye could see,
Saw the Vision of the world,
    and all the wonder that would be;
Saw the heavens fill with commerce,
    argosies of magic sails,
Pilots of the purple twilight,
    dropping down with costly bales;
Heard the heavens fill with shouting,
    and there rain'd a ghastly dew
From the nation's airy navies
    grappling in the central blue.

Against the background of such forebodings, it is ironical that the Wright brothers, after their pioneer flights in December 1903, met with initial skepticism when they tried to interest the governments of the United States and the European powers in their airplane. In military circles the Wrights' performances were dismissed as interesting but valueless circus stunts (McFarland, 1959). The significance of the airplane was better recognized outside the halls of government. In *The War in the Air*, written in 1908, H.G. Wells foresaw that the airplane would revolutionize the conduct and social consequences of war. He characterized air war as a 'universal guerilla war, a war inextricably involving civilians and homes and all the apparatus of social life' (quoted in Emme, 1959: 5).

When World War I broke out, aviation was still in its rudimentary stage: 'The pilots of the day were sportsmen, leaning a little towards madness, and there was no knowledge ... of what may be termed military flight, or of the possibilities of using aircraft as weapons of war' (Bishop, 1944: 29–30). The war, however, entailed a great boost to all phases of aviation development on both sides of the Atlantic. In the words of American Secretary of War Baker: 'Ten times as many years would not have produced the same advance if the years had been devoted to peaceful pursuits and commercial uses of airplanes had been the only incentive to investors and producers' (Kuhn, 1920: 369n). Thus, 'air power, unlike sea power, did not first evolve from the commercial use of a new means of transportation. It was born in war and only nurtured in peacetime' (Emme, 1959: 100).

The fact that the airplane was invented and perfected in an era of war and rampant nationalism gave prominence to the relationship between military aviation and government support of commercial air transport.

Hence state governments became the principal actors in early aviation. Technical factors leading to high costs made airlines uneconomic by ordinary market standards. Governments were willing to support them for a variety of reasons. For the European colonial powers the need to maintain rapid and adequate communication and transport ties with overseas colonies was a major concern. In the United States the first government involvement occurred in the form of airmail contracts with private operators beginning in 1916, and all American international routes before 1938 were pioneered under foreign airmail contracts. In brief, the reasons for the original government interest and intervention in civil aviation can be grouped under four rubrics (cf. Lissitzyn, 1942: 38–93; Wheatcroft, 1964: 46–57; Thornton, 1971: 192–7).

(1) *National defense*. World War I demonstrated beyond doubt the military value of aviation. The links between civil and military aviation also became well understood. First, civil aircraft in those days could easily be converted to military use. In addition, there were mutually advantageous personnel links between civil and military aviation. Immediately after World War I, for instance, most of the personnel employed in civil air transport consisted of demobilized and reserve military aviators.

(2) *Economic considerations*. Means of communication and transportation have always been considered as 'public services,' offering economic advantages to a state even if they may not be particularly profitable. The social values of aviation were especially evident to countries with vast territories and less developed hinterlands (the United States, Australia and the Soviet Union being cases in point). In the case of international aviation, foreign exchange earnings and balance-of-payments considerations provided additional economic incentives for government engagement.

(3) *Safety*. Governments everywhere regarded the safety of air transport operations as their special concern and responsibility and therefore established safety standards,

provided for the inspection and licensing of airline equipment and personnel, supplied air navigation aids, and so on.

(4) *Foreign policy considerations.* Since international aviation provides ample opportunities to 'show the flag' around the world, it has from the outset been viewed as enhancing the prestige of states. Air transport also facilitated propaganda and cultural penetration abroad.

Given the importance of aviation as an instrument of economic, military, and foreign policy, it is not surprising that the air transport industry from its infancy was subjected to more extensive government controls than other means of communication.

Air transportation, a delicate child born thanks to the technical progress made by aviation during the First World War, was the object, during its first years of existence, of much more attentive care by its parents, the sovereign States, than its older brothers and sisters — shipping, stage coach services, and the railways — had ever received. (Legrez, 1982: 147.)

Governments exercised control over aviation through regulation and through participation in the ownership or management of airlines. International carriers, in particular, were government-owned in part or in full. The privately owned US airlines seemed the only exceptions; yet, because of their dependence on heavy government subsidization, it seems reasonable to conclude that 'from their inception in the late 1920s through the immediate post-World War II period international airlines were essentially government enterprises' (Thornton, 1971: 191).

Air warfare played a decisive role in World War II, culminating with the atomic bomb, and the progress in aeronautical knowledge was even greater than in World War I.

Private flying practically disappeared as did the great majority of international commercial air operations. But this did not slow up the growth of transport flying. Quite the reverse. Transport by air soon became the normal means of wartime long-distance travel. At first a few, then hundreds, then thousands of transport aircraft were pressed into service. Worldwide air transport moved forward a generation in a few years. (Cooper, 1947: 158.)

Therefore, the interrelation of military and civil aviation was heavily emphasized immediately after the war. A 1945 report to the US Secretary of War by the Commanding General of the Army Air Forces (quoted in Emme, 1959: 313) is representative in this regard:

No activity having to do with aviation in any form can be considered as being completely independent of national security. Civil aviation must be encouraged both internally and internationally, and all arrangements, plans, agreements, and operations should be carried out with due regard for their military implications.

While government interest in international aviation has not diminished since World War II, it has changed character. Governments remain prepared to protect their national carriers. But whereas the linkage between military security and civil aviation was still an overriding concern of governments in the years following the end of World War II, it has since declined in urgency and importance. Increasing specialization has meant that commercial aircraft can no longer readily be converted to military use, except for transport of supplies. Nor has civil aviation contributed to the development of military air forces by acting as training grounds for military personnel or by perfecting aircraft design. Instead the reverse has occurred (Thornton, 1970: 81). Military training is a common background for airline pilots, and military aircraft policy has largely dictated the types of vehicles available to the airlines, as aircraft manufacturers draw on the experience of military designs (cf. Brooks, 1961: 141). The evolution of civil aviation is therefore to a great extent conditional on the continued production and development of military aviation. Military contracts are vital for the survival of leading aircraft manufacturers. In the 1970s the US aerospace companies suffered severe setbacks resulting from the reduction in military spending after the Vietnam War, the cutback in space expenditure, and the recession in the civilian economy. As other markets declined, military exports gained in importance (cf. Hoagland, 1978; Kaldor, 1979).

The number of international airlines has multiplied since World War II. Moreover, airlines gradually became less dependent on their governments for financial support. In the

1950s and 1960s traffic increased at an annual rate of 15 to 20 percent, at the same time as technological advances ensured declining operating costs. As a result, the airlines emerged from their subsidy cocoons as increasingly independent and economically viable actors. By 1957 more passengers crossed the Atlantic by air than by sea, and already in 1962 air passengers numbered more than twice as many as sea travellers across the Atlantic (Sampson, 1985: 139). Sir George Cayley's prediction in 1809 that air transport would overtake sea transport was coming true. Whereas air traffic across the Atlantic was doubling every five years, transatlantic liners would never again become economic.

Despite their economic success and global operations, international airlines by and large retained their national identity, the only significant exceptions being a few multinational carriers such as SAS and Air Afrique. Furthermore, international airlines continued to be wholly or predominantly government owned.

In summary, international aviation is an issue-area which from its inception has displayed a dynamic interaction of 'the pursuit of wealth' and 'the pursuit of power.' At the same time as it is linked to many important economic and ecological issue-areas or 'cobwebs' such as energy, balance of payments and environmental protection, it also engages the sovereignty, security and national prestige of states to a greater degree than most economic issue-areas. Civil aviation is one example of high-technology politico-economic issue-areas, where interdependence implies not only the mutual dependence of states but also the mutual dependence of civil and military sectors. Thus, the 'realist' criticism that regime studies have been preoccupied with 'low politics' does not apply to international aviation which lies at the intersection of 'high politics' and 'low politics.'

## The plan of this book

In Chapter 1 the basic concepts and explanatory modes of extant studies of international regimes are introduced and discussed. After identifying the sequence of international aviation regimes during our century in Chapter 2, I go on to apply prevalent explanatory models of regime dynamics to the air transport issue-area in Chapter 3.

The remainder of the book is devoted to an attempt at developing a complementary mode of explanation — one which focusses on the *process* of regime change, as distinct from the structural models that have dominated theoretical efforts to date. Chapter 4 outlines the basic features of a process perspective, emphasizing bargaining and organizational context. Subsequently, in Chapters 5 through 7, this perspective is applied to three instances of regime creation, change and persistence in international aviation: the drafting of multilateral conventions after World Wars I and II, and the US challenge to the existing regime in the late 1970s and early 1980s. After an assessment of the relative potency and interrelationships of different explanations of regime dynamics in the concluding chapter, I discuss the implications of my findings for the study of international regimes in other issue-areas.

Empirically, the main questions pursued in this essay are: Which regimes can be identified in the international aviation issue-area? And how can regime formation and trans-formation be accounted for? The theoretical problematique that I address in my case study of international air transport concerns the applicability and scope of extant theories of regime dynamics. Do they provide satisfactory and ex-haustive explanations of regime change and maintenance? What complements, if any, are needed?

# 1 Studying international regimes and regime change

The international political system is traditionally labelled anarchic, in the sense that it lacks a central authority. Although anarchy does not necessarily imply lack of order (Young, 1978: 242), the international system is often described as a Hobbesian state of nature in contrast to the legal order of national societies. With the rediscovery of international political economy among political scientists in the wake of the 1973–4 oil crisis — or oil 'shock,' as the Japanese aptly call it — this perspective has been modified. As the attention of scholars has shifted from the military-security aspects of international relations to international political economy, issue-based 'regimes' and the ensuing international orders have become new foci of study.

Students of international regimes address questions such as 'how islands of order can form in an ocean of disorder' (Haas, 1980: 385) and 'how . . . patterns of rule-guided policy coordination emerge, maintain themselves, and decay in world politics' (Keohane, 1984: 51). In the same vein, this study attempts to describe and explain the formation and transformation of international regimes in the issue-area of international civil air transport. It will draw on, and at the same time complement, extant theories of regime dynamics.

## International regimes

The word 'regime' evokes different associations among different people. The French word *'régime'* in everyday language means a diet — a purposive plan of eating, exercising and living, imposed by some medical or other authority. The word also has a political meaning: the government or rulership of a society. In this sense, it is often used pejoratively: the 'ancien regime,' the 'Franco regime' (Strange, 1982: 486). When used by international lawyers, the concept of an 'international regime' connotes a recognized set of *rules* agreed upon by states (Haas, 1980: 396). Political scientists build upon the legal concept in their understanding of 'international regimes,' but have broadened its meaning to include informal and even tacit agreements on substance as well as procedure.

An international regime has thus been loosely defined as 'principles, norms, rules, and decision-making procedures around which actor expectations converge in a given issue-area' (Krasner, 1982a: 185). The principles of regimes define the purposes that their adherents are expected to pursue. Norms define legitimate and illegitimate behavior in terms of responsibilities and obligations. Rules are more specific prescriptions or proscriptions for action. And the decision-making procedures of regimes are prevailing practices for implementing their principles and making collective choices (Krasner, 1982a: 186; Keohane, 1984: 57–8).

The regime concept, as applied to the international system, obviously has little in common with its domestic counterpart which suggests a recognized locus of power. In fact, this is one of the criticisms levied against the use of the regime concept internationally: 'The analogy with national governments implied by the use of the word regime ... is inherently false. It consequently holds a highly distorting mirror to reality' (Strange, 1982: 487). Yet, as long as one avoids associations with domestic regimes (as international lawyers have long done successfully), the notion of international regimes is a useful shorthand for the observable 'islands of order' in the international 'ocean of disorder.'

An international regime is obviously less than a global order and more than *ad hoc* agreements. Regimes may be thought of as intermediary normative frameworks which facilitate the making of substantial agreements in a given issue-area (Keohane, 1982: 337). As understood by political scientists (but not by international lawyers), they vary with respect to explicitness, formalization and adherence. They can be based on written legal documents or tacit, informal understandings; and they may encompass all or a limited number of states.

It should be noted that international regimes are basically subjective, attitudinal phenomena: 'they exist primarily as participants' understandings, expectations or convictions about legitimate, appropriate or moral behavior' (Puchala & Hopkins, 1982: 246).

Issue-areas — another component of the suggested definition of international regimes — may also be understood in subjective terms. Issues are separate items on the international agenda. The linking of issues into issue-areas is not inherent in international subject-matters but a human artifact which varies over time and across actors. 'When governments active on a set of issues see them as closely interdependent, and deal with them collectively, we call that set of issues an issue area' (Keohane & Nye, 1977: 65). In fact, the division into specialized departments in national governments is recognition of the fact that certain issues tend to appear together, and implies operational definitions of issue-areas. Thus 'sets of issues that are in fact dealt with in common negotiations and by the same, or closely coordinated, bureaucracies' (Keohane, 1984: 61) can be regarded as issue-areas.

Ocean management offers a good illustration of the subjective, changing and controversial character of international issue-areas. The oceans are used to fish, navigate, fight wars, extract oil and other resources, deposit waste, and conduct research. Until recently, each issue was dealt with separately. With the opening of the United Nations Law of the Sea Conference in 1971 under the premise that the oceans were to be considered 'the common heritage of mankind,' the whole cluster of issues came to be treated together as an issue-area. At the same time, disagreements arose, especially between rich and poor countries, over the boundaries of the oceans issue-area (cf. Keohane & Nye, 1977: 86–98; Haas, 1980: 365–7).

Regimes are something more than temporary cooperative arrangements. Yet just as perceptions of the boundaries of issue-areas change over time, so do regimes. Several regime studies have explored the evolution or life cycles of specific international regimes and have formulated general theories about regime change. A regime change is said to involve alteration of principles and norms. Changes in rules and

decision-making procedures, on the other hand, are referred
to as changes within regimes; incoherence among a regime's
principles, norms, rules and procedures or inconsistency
between the regime and actual behavior implies the weaken-
ing of a regime (Krasner, 1982a: 187–9).

Various explanations of regime formation and change have
been suggested. In the following section I shall discuss
different explanatory modes found in the literature.

## Explaining regime formation and change

A first distinction can be made between *normative* and
*empirical* approaches to the study of regime evolution. Ex-
ponents of the normative approach, sometimes labelled
'idealists' (Bergesen, 1984: 9–12) or 'evolutionary holists'
(Haas, 1980: 359), argue that key perceptions concerning
welfare, equity and the quality of life are changing rapidly and
will have to change further in order to save this endangered
planet. Scholars in this tradition strive to specify desirable
regimes. The so-called 'world-order' school is representative
of this approach (see Mendlovitz, 1975; Falk, 1977).

Since my task is essentially empirical (to identify and
explain regime evolution in the international aviation issue-
area) rather than normative (to outline desirable aviation
regimes), I shall in the following concentrate on various
empirical approaches. Different aspects of reality have been
suggested by students of international regimes as relevant for
explaining regime formation and change. First, one may
distinguish between *economic* and *political* explanations.

Economic modes of explanation see regime evolution as
adaptation to new volumes and new forms of transnational
economic activity. New regimes emerge, as non-regime
situations or old regimes prove inadequate to cope with
increased and diversified transactions (Keohane & Nye, 1977:
40). Among those economic factors which have been suggested as accounting for regime evolution, I shall single out
two: *technological change* and *change in supply and demand.*

Behind the unprecedented economic growth in the industrialized world and the rapid increase in world trade after
World War II lie remarkable technological advances. Of

special relevance to the present undertaking is the dramatic progress in transportation and communications technology, which has reduced the costs of distance.

Another type of explanation focusses on supply/demand dynamics. Specifically, *surplus capacity* as a result of increased supply and/or decreased demand has been proposed as a source of regime change. 'When many important nations face a sustained, severe problem in a sector, a problem that stems from large amounts of excess capacity for production, a situation of "surplus capacity" exists' (Cowhey & Long, 1983: 162). Such a situation is assumed to contain pressures for regime change. More specifically, surplus capacity is seen to erode liberal regimes (Cowhey & Long, 1983: 162–5).

The favored political mode of explanation has been *structural*: regime change results from changes in the structure of international power. A 'realist' version of this theory emphasizes changes in the overall power structure, predicting a strong tendency toward congruence among issue-areas. As the global overall power structure changes, so will most regimes based on the previous distribution of power (Keohane & Nye, 1977: 42–9). In its 'neorealist' version, the structuralist argument hinges on 'issue structure' and 'issue-specific power': different issue-areas are assumed to have different power structures, and power bases in one issue-area are not necessarily effective when applied to others. Therefore, no congruence is to be expected across issue-areas.

In either of its varieties, the structural mode of explanation has tended to rely on a theory of hegemonic stability. The two central propositions of this theory are: (1) that international regimes are typically created by a single dominant power, a hegemon; and (2) that the maintenance of regimes requires continued hegemony (Keohane, 1984: 31). 'Fragmentation of power between competing countries leads to fragmentation of the international economic regime; concentration of power contributes to stability' (Keohane, 1980: 136). Hegemonic distributions of power are assumed to lead to stable regimes, because the hegemon has the capability to maintain the regimes and to provide the collective goods needed to make the regime function effectively. Conversely, under conditions of declining hegemony regimes will weaken.

The hegemonic stability theory has been applied, in

particular, to the evolution of postwar economic regimes. The creation of strong and stable regimes after World War II, such as the Bretton Woods regime in the monetary issue-area and the GATT regime in international trade, is attributable to American economic strength and leadership; and the erosion of these regimes since the 1970s reflects the decline of American economic power, according to this interpretation. Thus, one prominent exponent of this theory, Charles Kindleberger, makes the following diagnosis of today's political economy (1981: 253):

I conclude that the danger we face is not too much power in the international economy, but too little, not an excess of domination, but a superfluity of would-be free riders, unwilling to mind the store, and waiting for a storekeeper to appear. No place, to quote President Truman, for the buck to stop. I say this without implication that there is any threat to the world economic system from outside. But without a stabilizer, the system in my judgment is unstable.

Structuralism generally predicts that significant shifts in the balance of power and erosions of hegemonic stability will occur in the wake of major wars. Thus, Robert Gilpin argues that the 'right to rule' on the part of a hegemon rests primarily on its victory in the last hegemonic war:

The great turning points in world history have been provided by these hegemonic struggles among political rivals; these periodic conflicts have reordered the international system and propelled history in new and unchartered directions. They resolve the question of which state will govern the system, as well as what ideas and values will predominate, thereby determining the ethos of succeeding ages. The outcome of these wars affect the economic, social, and ideological structures of individual societies as well as the structure of the larger international system. (Gilpin, 1981: 203.)

Regimes established on the basis of any postwar balance of power are predestined to change eventually, according to Gilpin (1981: 210), because 'the conclusion of one hegemonic war is the beginning of another cycle of growth, expansion, and eventual decline.'

A different explanatory mode is represented by what

Robert Keohane (1984) labels 'functional' theories of regime creation and change. These explanations are *post hoc* in character, they account for regimes in terms of *anticipated* effects or functions. Regimes are thus assumed to emerge 'as ways to overcome the deficiencies that make it impossible to consummate even mutually beneficial agreements' (Keohane, 1984: 83).

To avoid the ambiguity and teleological implications of the term 'function,' I shall instead refer to *situational* explanations. This means that the question I pursue is 'What kind of situations trigger the creation and revision of regimes?' rather than 'What functions do regimes perform?'

In general, cooperation between egoistic actors in the absence of any superior authority grows out of situations which are frequently characterized as dilemmas, as either/or choices between incompatible alternatives where neither alternative is optimal but each has both desirable and undesirable consequences (cf. Stenelo, 1984: 160–2). Thus international politics scholars have pointed to the continual 'security dilemma' facing states in an anarchic international system: 'many of the means by which a state tries to increase its security decrease the security of others' (Jervis, 1978: 169). Economic theories of 'market failure' and the 'free-rider' problem in the provision of collective goods analyze dilemma situations among economic actors. And the game-theoretical 'prisoners' dilemma' has been used by different disciplines as an allegory for a variety of social situations. These different approaches are related, the common denominator being the individual actors' choice between cooperation and defection from common action (Stein, 1982: 304–8).

The prisoners' dilemma game is an archetypical formulation of the choice between cooperation and defection. The game owes its name to an anecdote about two prisoners charged with the same crime who are held incommunicado. If both confess, both will be convicted. If neither confesses, neither will be convicted. But if one confesses while the other keeps silent, the first not only goes free but gets a reward to boot, whereas the second gets a more severe punishment than he would have got if both confessed. Another example of the same game structure may be even more illuminative and pertinent to the evolution of cooperation among egoists:

Assume you possess large quantities of some item (money, for example) and want to obtain some amount of another item (stamps, groceries, diamonds). You arrange a mutually agreeable trade with the only dealer of that item known to you. You are both satisfied with the amounts you will be giving and getting. For some reason, though, the exchange must take place in secret. Each of you agrees to leave a bag at a designated place in the woods and to pick up the other's bag at the other's designated place. Suppose it is clear to both of you that you will never meet or have further dealings with each other again. Clearly there is something for each of you to fear, namely that the other one will leave an empty bag. Obviously if you both leave full bags, you will both be satisfied, but equally obviously it is even more satisfying to get something for nothing. You are therefore tempted to leave an empty bag. (Hofstadter, 1983: 14.)

*[margin handwritten note: not the case in reality in IR.]*

To defect is each actor's dominant strategy in prisoners' dilemma, and the defect-defect (DD) solution is the equilibrium outcome, if the game is played only once. Even if cooperation is the actors' first choice, they may not be able to reach the cooperation-cooperation (CC) solution, as the situation of the hunters in Rousseau's 'Stag Hunt' illustrates: 'If they cooperate to trap the stag, they will all eat well. But if one person defects to chase a rabbit — which he likes less than stag — none of the others will get anything' (Jervis, 1978: 167). Although each hunter realizes that collaboration maximizes everybody's gain, there is always the temptation to make a grab for a *sure* meal, a rabbit. In his analysis of 'Stag Hunt' as an analogy for the security dilemma of states, Robert Jervis (1978: 168) points out that 'unless each person thinks that the others will cooperate, he himself will not'; therefore, 'although actors may know that they seek a common goal, they may not be able to reach it.' The game theory matrices for prisoners' dilemma and 'Stag Hunt' are given in Figure 1, with the numbers in the boxes representing the order of the actors' preferences.

Economic theories of market failure and collective goods deal with similar dilemmas. Market failure refers to situations in which market forces fail to result in optimal solutions. The market for used cars is frequently used as an illustration:

... owners of defective cars ('lemons') have a greater incentive to sell their vehicles than do owners of 'creampuffs.' Since prospective

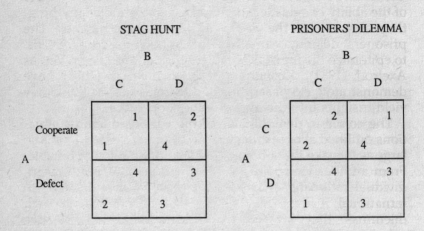

**Figure 1.** Stag Hunt and Prisoners' Dilemma

buyers know that they are unable reliably to determine when a used car is a 'lemon,' they will insist on paying less than the real value of a good-quality used car, in order to adjust for the risk they run of being stuck with a sour one. As a result, owners of good used cars will be unable to sell them for their real value and may therefore be unwilling to sell them at the discounted price that the market will bear. (Keohane, 1984: 82.)

Because of this 'quality uncertainty,' buyers and sellers will be unable to consummate some mutually profitable deals.

The suboptimal provision of collective goods is assumed to stem from the individual actor's incentive to be a 'free rider.' Thus, 'under certain conditions, the problem of collective goods is a classic prisoners' dilemma in which each individual is better off not contributing to the provision of a collective good, but in which the equilibrium outcome of everyone's deciding to be a free rider is a world in which all are worse off than if they had contributed equally to the provision of the good' (Stein, 1982: 307).

What, then, is the relevance of these representations of dilemma situations to the creation of international regimes? On the face of it, these theories seem to draw a gloomy picture of the ability of egoistic individuals to cooperate; if anything, they may explain the *absence* of international regimes. The prisoners' dilemma game has indeed been used by 'realists' to epitomize the inevitability of conflict among states. Yet, as Axelrod (1984), Keohane (1984), and Jervis (1978) have demonstrated, closer scrutiny of dilemmas such as these may yield insights into the evolution of cooperation.

The common denominator of the various dilemma situations outlined above is that the temptation to defect looms so large as to make the suboptimal DD solution highly probable. From another viewpoint, these situations illustrate that individual rationality may lead to collective irrationality. International regimes may be seen as a response to such dilemmas; they are 'created to deal with the collective suboptimality that can emerge from individual behavior' (Stein, 1982: 307). But how can egoistic individuals overcome their temptation to defect?

It obviously makes a difference whether these dilemmas are faced once or repeatedly. Let us return for a moment to the aforementioned prisoners' dilemma metaphor and alter its time horizon:

Suppose both you and the dealer very much want to have a regular supply of what the other has to offer, and so before conducting your first exchange you agree to carry on a lifelong exchange once a month . . . Now, what do you do on your first exchange? Bringing an empty bag seems fairly nasty as the opening of a relationship; hardly an effective way to build up trust. Suppose you bring a full bag and the dealer brings one too. All is bliss — for a month. Then you both must go back. Will your next bag be empty or full? (Hofstadter, 1983: 14.)

In multiple-play or 'iterated' prisoners' dilemma the short-run gains of defection are normally outweighed by the long-run losses of mutual defection. In Robert Axelrod's (1984: 174) words:

For cooperation to prove stable, the future must have a sufficiently large shadow. This means that the importance of the next encounter between the same two individuals must be great enough to make defection an unprofitable strategy when the other player is provocable. It requires that the players have a large enough chance of meeting again and that they do not discount the significance of their next meeting too greatly.

If prisoners' dilemma is repeated indefinitely, it begins to resemble 'Stag Hunt' with a solution (CC) which is in the best interest of all the participants (Jervis, 1978: 171). The temptation to defect in 'Stag Hunt' is, in turn, diminished, if the 'shadow of the future' is sufficiently long:

If the hunters are a permanent group, and expect to hunt together again, the immediate gains from unilateral defection relative to unrequited cooperation must be balanced against the cost of diminished cooperation in the future. In both Prisoners' Dilemma and Stag Hunt, defection in the present *decreases* the likelihood of cooperation in the future. In both, therefore, iteration improves the prospects for cooperation. (Oye, 1985: 14.)

The dilemmas outlined above represent *bargaining situations*, that is, situations characterized by the coincidence of cooperative and conflictual elements, interdependent decisions, and uncertainty as to how the other actor(s) will behave. Examples of bargaining situations, thus defined, abound in all aspects of social life. The superpower relationship of 'mutual deterrence' is a case in point, as well as such everyday situations as driving a car through a busy intersection without traffic lights.

Bargaining situations typically provide bases for negotiations. While a discussion of negotiation dynamics as explanations of regime creation and change will be deferred to Chapter 4, the argument thus far suggests the following proposition: In a bargaining situation characterized by a 'dilemma of common interests' (Stein, 1982) in an issue-area which requires continuous negotiations, an international regime may provide a normative and institutional framework for future negotiations.

What, then, increases or decreases the likelihood that such a bargaining situation will usher in a new international regime? A regime, it will be recalled, represents a CC solution in the game matrices above. The chances of arriving at this outcome will be enhanced (1) if the incentives to cooperate are increased, as a result either of heightened gains of mutual cooperation (CC) or of diminished costs of CD; (2) if the incentives to defect are decreased, as a result either of diminished gains of DC or of increased costs of DD (cf. Jervis, 1978: 171). In other words, the actors are more likely to agree on a regime, the more they win and the less they risk by cooperating, on the one hand; and the less they win and the more they risk by defecting, on the other.

Translated to international relations, such changes in the payoff structure are likely to occur in the wake of major wars. To that extent, the situational model coincides with the structural one. But structural and situational models point to wars as catalysts of regime change for different reasons. For structuralism, wars are significant because they tend to give rise to major shifts in the existing balance of power. The situational perspective, on the other hand, emphasizes changes in the perceived advantages of cooperation and disadvantages of non-cooperation or 'defection' that tend to occur as a result of war experiences. Wars dramatically demonstrate the costs of interstate conflict, and the yearning for cooperative arrangements becomes particularly strong after a devastating war.

The number of actors is another factor assumed to have an effect on the prospects for cooperation in dilemma-like situations. As the number of actors increases, (a) transactions and information costs rise; (b) defection becomes more likely, at the same time as recognition and control problems become more severe; and (c) the feasibility of sanctioning defectors diminishes (Oye, 1985: 19). Thus, the greater the number of involved actors, the more difficult the creation of an international regime is assumed to be.

In summary, situational theories indicate what kind of situations are likely to trigger, as well as what kind of situational changes will increase the likelihood of, the creation or transformation of international regimes.

Sometimes a special category of *cognitive* explanations is added to structural and situational ones. Beverly Crawford and Stefanie Lenway (1985: 399), for example, contrast structural and cognitive theories of regime change.

Theorists who have focused on structure have ignored the substance of participants' goals and the process by which policies can change, as well as the role of information in shaping participants' goals. Theorists who have focused on the cognitive aspects of regime change have not systematically investigated the way in which power relationships shape cognition and structure bargaining, or the way in which powerful actors can create constraints and incentives that change the behavior of others.

Ernst Haas is usually singled out as the leading exponent of cognitive regime explanations. Focussing on 'choice based on perception and cognition' and 'change in perception,' Haas (1980: 360, 361) contends that 'institutionalized collaboration can be explored in terms of the interaction between changing knowledge and changing social goals.' *Learning* plays a major role in Haas's framework. 'Building or changing a regime is a form of human problem-solving that requires actors to learn concepts' (Haas, 1982: 209).

The differences between structural and situational explanations, on the one hand, and cognitive explanations, on the other, should not be exaggerated. Haas's (1980: 360) own notion of regime evolution 'accepts the existence of power differentials and the importance of hierarchy among states — without sacrificing to such a view the possibility of choice based on perception and cognition inspired by additional calculations.' Conversely, Robert Keohane (1984: 132) argues that 'a structural analysis of constraints and a functional understanding of international regimes are both necessary to put the phenomenon of actor cognition into its proper political context.'

The obvious conclusion is that structural and situational theories, on the one hand, and cognitive theories, on the other, are complementary rather than mutually exclusive. In the realm of politics, what is 'real' is what men perceive to be real. Thus structural and situational factors become effective through the mediation of actor cognitions. Changes in the power structure and the emergence of bargaining situations, *as perceived by the principal actors*, explain the evolution of international regimes. Therefore, I shall not treat cognitive theories as a separate mode of explanation but rather include actor cognitions in my subsequent discussion of structural and situational factors accounting for regime change in international aviation.

Let us turn, now, to a consideration of regime evolution in the issue-area of international air transport in Chapter 2, and then see in Chapter 3 to what extent regime change can be accounted for by economic and political, structural and situational theories.

# 2 Regime evolution in international aviation

The first *international* flight took place in 1909 when the French pilot Louis Blériot crossed the Channel from France to England (Cooper, 1947: 17), and the first *commercial* air service was an airmail flight in Britain from Blackpool to Southport the following year (Corbett, 1965: 26). But 'until the outbreak of World War I, ... the aeroplane was regarded by most authorities, both technical and business, as of potential use only for sporting or military purposes' (Davies, 1964: 3). Count Zeppelin's Deutsche Luftschiffahrt Aktien-Gesellschaft, DELAG, which carried more than 35,000 passengers some 170,000 miles from 1910 to 1914, may claim to have been the world's first scheduled passenger air service (Gibbs-Smith, 1967: 35; Davies, 1964: 5). And the French Farman company, which flew its bi-planes with fourteen passengers between London and Paris and between Brussels and Paris, could claim in 1919 to be the first international airline (Sampson, 1985: 29). Yet it was only after World War I that regular international air commerce began.

International routes were first established in the countries of Western Europe where, as a result of their limited geographic area, aircraft had to cross national boundaries in order to be used economically. In the United States, where the first demand was for internal routes across its vast territory, international airline services were not inaugurated until almost ten years after those in Europe (Cooper, 1947: 152).

The interwar years were a great pioneering period, crowned by the opening of regular transatlantic air services in 1939. Thus, by the outbreak of World War II, most major international routes had been established, and a network of airlines connected the continents (cf. Lissitzyn, 1942: 4–5).

The era after World War II has witnessed a revolutionary development in international aviation. Since the 1940s total passenger traffic has expanded forty times, and there are seven times as many flights by aircraft ten times the size (Dargan, 1976: 1). International airlines carry over one hundred million passengers, some seven million tons of cargo, and eight billion pieces of mail a year on an integrated network covering three thousand airports in virtually all nations of the globe (Hammarskjöld, 1978a).

Turning to an exploration of the political aspects of this dynamic issue-area, the international aviation system over the years has undergone modifications that may be analyzed in terms of regime changes.

## The 'unrestricted sovereignty' regime, 1919–1944

In the field of aviation, the creation of norms and rules began early. 'Whereas as a general rule the practice of states determines doctrine, this has not been the case in aviation, where thought about the rules which should govern air communications started before air communications actually existed' (Goedhuis, 1942: 610). Also, international regulation preceded national or local legislation (Kuhn, 1920: 381).

Already by 1880, the Institute of International Law, a private association of eminent jurists from several countries, included the subject of aviation in its draft project on a convention for the laws and customs of war. The Hague Peace Conference of 1899 adopted a declaration agreeing 'for a term of five years' to 'forbid the discharge of projectiles and explosives from balloons or by other new methods of similar nature' (Colegrove, 1930: 42, 47).

In 1909, before Blériot's flight, the French government, as a result of the many unregulated balloon flights in Europe, called the world's first international aviation conference. In the summer of 1910 representatives of eighteen European countries convened in Paris. The Paris conference saw an early clash between opposing legal principles. On the one hand, there was the idea of the 'freedom of the air' modelled on Grotius' *mare liberum* doctrine. The principle of state sovereignty might, on the other hand, be extended to the airspace above a state's territory. In Paris the German and French delegations, headed by lawyers, argued in favor of extensive freedom of flight, whereas the British delegation, headed by an admiral, reasoned in terms of state sovereignty.

In the absence of agreement on the general principles of international aviation, the conference adjourned. Subsequent diplomatic exchanges were equally unsuccessful in reconciling the divergent positions, and the conference was never called back into session (Cooper, 1947: 18–20; Goedhuis, 1942: 598–9; Johnson, 1972: 220–3).

While jurists continued to debate theories of freedom of the air, the European governments acted to safeguard their airspace sovereignty in the wake of the Paris conference. The British Aerial Navigation Act, passed by Parliament in 1911 and amended in 1913, gave the Home Secretary complete power to regulate the entry of foreign aircraft and to prescribe zones over which foreign aircraft were not allowed to fly. Most of the channel coast of Britain soon became a prohibited zone. France and Germany, as well as other European states, followed suit and created expanding prohibited zones. In brief, the European political climate in the years prior to the outbreak of World War I induced governments to assign priority to military security considerations at the expense of theoretical freedom of the air (Cooper, 1947: 20–1; Johnson, 1972: 224–5). As war broke out in 1914, country after country in Europe declared its air boundaries closed. 'Political frontiers had been built in the airspace where physical boundaries could never be' (Cooper, 1947: 22).

The Peace Conference following World War I, assembling in Paris in the winter of 1918–19, faced two aviation problems: in addition to the specific question of the future of military and civil aviation in Germany and other defeated enemy states, the need to regulate international civil aviation in times of peace had become urgent. While there was early agreement to demilitarize Germany in the air, the issue of whether German civil aviation should be restricted caused differences of opinion. In the end the least restrictive American line won, and German civil aviation was permitted inside Germany. On the broader question of the regulation of peacetime international aviation, the Peace Conference adopted the so-called Paris Convention in late 1919. Its first article endows each state with 'complete and exclusive sovereignty over the airspace above its territory.' The territory of a state was understood as 'including the national territory, both that of the mother country and of the colonies, and the territorial waters adjacent thereto.'

Although the United States took a very active part in drafting the Paris Convention, the US Senate never ratified it, as the Convention was associated with the Versailles peace treaty and the League of Nations. The Soviet Union did not participate at Paris. Yet both the United States and the Soviet Union asserted the Paris principle of airspace sovereignty by national decree in the 1920s. Moreover, the United States in 1928 became one of the signatories of the Havana Convention, a multilateral convention for the Western Hemisphere modelled on that of 1919 (Cooper, 1947: 27–35; Johnson, 1972: 233–4; Lissitzyn, 1942: 366–73).

In short, the international aviation regime created after World War I rested on the *principle* of unrestricted state sovereignty. This implied the *norm* that each state have the ultimate power to decide on all air transport within its airspace. The principal *rule* guiding international air transport was thus that government approval must be acquired for overflight and landing. Given the extensive government control over aviation at that time, bilateral government negotiations became the main *decision-making procedure*. In order to establish an international air service, a state had to negotiate with the foreign governments concerned for the right to overfly and land.

The Paris Convention ushered in a period of intensive bilateral 'horse trading' (Cooper, 1947: 145) between governments for air rights. Negotiations were complicated by the adherence of most governments to the principle of *reciprocity* for the granting of air transport privileges and the frequent use of these privileges as weapons for gaining ends that had little to do with aviation. As a consequence, conflicts often occurred in the process of intergovernmental bargaining.

To mention but a few examples, Italy refused to grant landing rights to the British Imperial Airways on its eastbound flights, unless receipts on a certain run were divided equally with the weak and unprofitable Italian company. Turkey prohibited transit flights over its territory, thus depriving European services to southern Asia of the shortest route. Greece required all foreign airlines passing over its territory to land at Athens and to coordinate their schedules with those of the domestic Greek air services. Iran made difficulties about allowing Imperial Airways to use the most direct route to India over Iranian territory. In 1939 Spain reserved landing and transit rights to companies belonging to countries that had been allies of Franco during the civil war, and barred Imperial Airways, Air France, and KLM from flying over Spanish territory. By refusing to let foreign carriers use Hawaii as a base, the United States blocked Australian and Canadian plans for connecting air routes. Australia retaliated by denying US carriers similar rights (cf. Cooper, 1947: 145; Corbett, 1965: 29–30; Goedhuis, 1942: 603; Lissitzyn, 1942: 397–8; Smith, 1950: 128).

Transatlantic services provide good illustrations of the ways in which the early guarding of airspace sovereignty and insistence on reciprocity delayed the development of international air commerce. The United States had the capacity, but not the political right, to fly across the Atlantic by 1935. Pan American Airways reportedly entered into secret discussions with the British Imperial Airways as early as 1934. The British proposed a 50–50 division of North Atlantic traffic along with an agreement on 'spheres of influence,' excluding American aircraft from Europe and the Middle East in return for American predominance in South America and the Pacific (Berle, 1945: 3). After arduous negotiations, in 1937 Britain granted Pan American a permit to land in Newfoundland, England and Bermuda, conditional on the simultaneous initiation of transatlantic operations to the United States by Imperial Airways. As Imperial Airways for technical reasons was long unable to participate in such a service, it did not commence until the summer of 1939. Meanwhile, Portugal had granted the United States and Britain landing rights in the Azores, largely invalidated by the condition that Lisbon be the first and last stop of any transatlantic routes using the Azores; and Germany had acquired the capacity to begin regular operations across the Atlantic but did not obtain landing rights from the United States (Mance, 1943: 60–1; Cooper, 1947: 146–8; Lissitzyn, 1942: 400–2). The outbreak of war a few months after the delayed opening of the North

Atlantic route put an abrupt end to the interwar 'horse trading' for air rights.

## The 'Chicago-Bermuda' regime after World War II

In November 1944 — after the Bretton Woods conference but  ʜ
before the San Francisco conference — representatives of fifty-four states convened in Chicago upon the invitation of the US government to discuss the postwar planning of international civil aviation. American-British preliminary discussions in early 1944 had made it clear that agreement would be difficult to achieve. Therefore the conference was postponed until after the American 1944 presidential election, when the US government would have greater freedom of action. The Soviet Union did not participate at Chicago. Though invited, the Soviet Union withdrew at the last minute, ostensibly as a protest against the participation of certain pro-Fascist countries, such as Spain and Portugal (Lowenfeld, 1975: 37; Thornton, 1970: 20–2).

The old freedom versus sovereignty controversy re-emerged at Chicago but was not solved, even though various formulas were suggested by which national sovereignty and prerogatives might be combined with the need for a reasonably free international air commerce. The Chicago conference marked the beginning of a continuing discussion of different 'freedoms of the air' (cf. Figure 2).

The first two technical freedoms were established in the International Air Services Transit Agreement which was prepared by the Chicago conference and has since gained wide acceptance. This was a major improvement over the previous regime. No longer did states have to enter a series of bilateral negotiations for overflight rights to open new routes.

To realize what a landmark this is in aeronautical history one really needs to have lived with the subject during the years between the wars and to have seen at first-hand how firmly almost every state has repulsed any attempt to release international transport from its cocoon of multiple national restrictions. For the first time, nations which wish to trade with one another through the air can reach each other's territories without needing to meet the terms imposed separately by every state along the way. They are assured that, except for nonstop ocean crossings, they can halt for refueling at intervals which are economically desirable and will not have to carry enough fuel for roundabout flights. The participants to the transit agreement undertake to abstain from the role of feudal baron who levied private tribute on all the commerce passing along the highroads within his grasp. (Warner, 1945: 24–5.)

An International Air Transport Agreement covering five freedoms, promoted by the United States, was signed by only sixteen countries. As it could thus not be considered a basis for a worldwide aviation regime, the United States in 1946 renounced the agreement (Cooper, 1947: 174–7; Johnson, 1972: 258–9). In the absence of any effective multilateral arrangement, the fundamental third and fourth freedoms as well as the much-disputed fifth and sixth freedoms therefore remain subjects of bilateral bargaining. The sixth freedom was not discussed at Chicago but has since slowly become accepted.

Agreement was reached at Chicago to create an institution, the International Civil Aviation Organization (ICAO), which shortly became a specialized agency of the United Nations. Australia, New Zealand and Canada had submittted proposals for a world organization which would own and operate international airlines. ICAO, however, was set up primarily as a technical body, facilitating international collaboration in such matters as safety, navigation and standardization, not as a strong regulatory body of the kind envisaged by the Commonwealth countries or established in other politico-economic issue-areas around the same time, such as the IMF or GATT (Lowenfeld, 1975: 37).

Several other components necessary to an aviation regime — how to determine routes, capacity and fares — were left unresolved by the Chicago conference. The principal differences were between the United States, which in general advocated the free play of market forces, and European states headed by Britain, which favored strong government controls over these functions. A compromise formula to end the deadlock reached at Chicago was found two years later in the first postwar US-British bilateral aviation agreement concluded

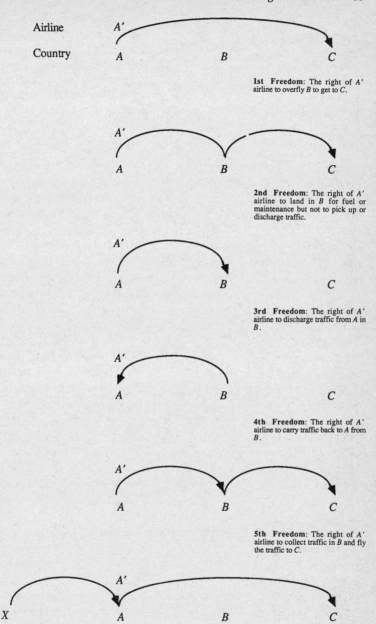

Airline

Country

**1st Freedom**: The right of *A'* airline to overfly *B* to get to *C*.

**2nd Freedom**: The right of *A'* airline to land in *B* for fuel or maintenance but not to pick up or discharge traffic.

**3rd Freedom**: The right of *A'* airline to discharge traffic from *A* in *B*.

**4th Freedom**: The right of *A'* airline to carry traffic back to *A* from *B*.

**5th Freedom**: The right of *A'* airline to collect traffic in *B* and fly the traffic to *C*.

**6th Freedom**: The right of *A'* airline to pick up traffic in *X* that is bound for *C* and route it through *A*. This traffic normally belongs to the airlines of *X* and *C*.

**Figure 2.** Six freedoms of the air

at Bermuda. This came to serve as a worldwide model for future bilateral agreements. The 1946 Bermuda agreement represented 'not merely a bilateral agreement between the two major air transport nations, but a general philosophy on the way in which the economic regulation of the industry should be achieved' (Wheatcroft, 1964: 70).

The Bermuda principles were, in brief, as follows: the *routes* to be operated between two countries are agreed in bilateral negotiations with individual government control over the designation of carriers to operate these routes; *capacity* and *frequency* levels (how big an aircraft is to operate a route and how frequently) are, in the first instance, to be left to the judgment of the operators themselves, subject to deliberately vague guidelines and *ex post facto* review if one party feels that its interests are being unduly affected; *fares* are negotiated by the airlines within the International Air Transport Association (IATA) framework, agreements being subject to approval by the governments of each country involved. It was agreed within the Bermuda principles that fares be uniform on the same route to avoid price and subsidy wars (see, e.g., Cooper, 1947: 177–8; Lowenfeld, 1975: 37–8; Thornton, 1970: 34–7; Lipman, 1976: 4–6; Wheatcroft, 1964: 70–1).

In sum, the Chicago-Bermuda regime diluted the *principle* of airspace sovereignty by combining it with the partially contradictory principle of international regulation. The notion of 'six freedoms,' like the principle of sovereignty, implies the *norm* that nations have some claims on traffic originating in their country. This provides a basis for the argument that a national carrier has a basic right to a 50 percent share of the traffic on routes to and from the home country, an argument that is frequently used by weaker countries in bilateral negotiations (Wassenbergh, 1970: 7–16; Harbison, 1982: 49). At the same time, the Bermuda agreement implies a norm of multilateralism, especially as far as fare-setting is concerned.

The Bermuda agreement also provided a set of *rules* concerning the establishment and operation of international routes and, in addition, outlined the *decision-making procedures* to be followed. The 1919–39 pattern of bilateral government negotiations was superseded by a hybrid pattern of decision-making. Traffic rights and route structures continued to be subjects of bilateral government negotiations, yet the gradual acceptance of certain 'freedoms of the air' attenuated the previously prevalent conflict element of these negotiations. As under the 1919 regime, the principle of reciprocity guided bilateral negotiations. But this principle came to be applied in a less restrictive and stifling fashion than in the interwar years. Reciprocity in aviation negotiations, as in most other international negotiations, implies a notion of 'fair exchange,' of contingency and equivalence (cf. Keohane, 1986). The typical method of bilateral air transport negotiations under the Chicago-Bermuda regime has been described by an American negotiator thus (quoted in Harbison, 1982: 49): 'First, the governments sat down to trade commercial air rights for commercial air rights ... Second, the negotiators aimed at an exchange of air rights which had an approximately equal value for each side.'

The fare structure of international routes was left to the airlines to work out within the framework of the IATA traffic conferences, and the government review of IATA agreements came increasingly to assume the character of rubber stamp approval. IATA evolved into a forum for extensive airline cooperation in such matters as building a global scheduling, reservations and communication system, standardizing tickets and carrier/location codes, allowing travellers to book complex interline routings while paying a fixed charge in one currency ('clearing house'), and coordinating airport handling of passengers, baggage, cargo and mail (see, e.g., Brancker, 1977).

## An aborted attempt at regime change

Having survived for more than three decades, the Chicago-Bermuda regime — especially its 'Bermuda leg' — came under increasing attack in the latter half of the 1970s. A renewed battle emerged between 'liberals' insisting on competition and deregulation and 'conservatives' insisting on regulation and restrictions for international aviation.

In June 1976, the British government denounced the Bermuda agreement with twelve-months' notice within which to negotiate a new agreement or terminate the existing one. The British felt that US carriers were benefiting more from the Bermuda agreement than British carriers. In particular, the fifth-freedom rights of the US carriers to fly traffic beyond London to almost every city of importance caused British complaints. After extended negotiations a new bilateral agreement — Bermuda II — was signed in July 1977, which accorded several new routes to the British carriers and limited the fifth-freedom rights of the US carriers, while permitting them to carry passengers originating in the United States beyond London to any point in Europe. Among 'liberals' in the United States, the new agreement was considered in many ways more restrictive than Bermuda I (Thomka-Gazdik, 1982: 288).

Around the same time, ICAO, which until then had been mainly concerned with technical and safety matters, got actively involved in the economic regulation of international air transport, prompted by Third World countries (Haanappel, 1983: 167). A Special Air Transport Conference was convened in April 1977. While giving provisional support to the existing IATA decision-making procedures for rate-making, the ICAO conference envisaged the possibility of increased government involvement (cf. Recommendations 10, 11, ICAO, 1977). In other words, the 'liberals' seemed to have lost the first round of the battle.

However, in late 1977 United States international aviation policy took a new direction, partly as a reaction to Bermuda II. In the words of President Carter, the central American goal should henceforth be 'to move toward a truly competitive system' where 'market forces should be the main determinant of the variety, quality and price of air services' (quoted in Harbison, 1982: 1). The new policy amounted to a fervent call for international 'deregulation,' emphasizing competition, liberalization of charter operations, no capacity restraints and 'marketplace' pricing with minimal government involvement.

There were strong commercial incentives behind the American posture. Especially on the vital North Atlantic routes, the US carriers' market share was being steadily eroded. In addition, President Carter had good political reasons for his policy, having been elected on a platform which included reduced government regulation and involvement generally in the marketplace. The deregulation of domestic American air transport, already initiated under the Ford administration, had furthermore set a powerful precedent.

US efforts to implement the new policy included, first, the denunciation and renegotiation of a number of bilateral agreements. In these negotiations the United States pressed for 'liberal' agreements, characterized by greater reliance on 'market forces' in determining capacity, frequency, entry and pricing. American negotiators demanded 'multiple permissive route awards' (allowing a multitude of carriers to enter and leave routes at will), unilateral low-fare pricing, and agreement on country-of-origin charter rules. To induce other states to accept their terms, the American negotiators promised to open new routes and long-sought US gateways to foreign carriers, and threatened to divert American traffic to neighboring countries.

Some twenty 'liberal' bilateral agreements have been concluded. All of these include pricing articles which restrict governmental powers to reject airline price proposals. The most common clause calls for 'double disapproval': unless both affected governments agree, the price cannot be rejected. A less extreme 'country-of-origin' version permits governments to reject prices on traffic originating in their own territory (cf. Harbison, 1982).

The second prong of the US attack on the existing international aviation regime consisted of an open challenge to IATA's central role under the Chicago-Bermuda formula. The American acceptance of the IATA fare-setting framework since 1945 rests formally on exemption from US antitrust laws. On 9 June 1978, the US Civil Aeronautics Board (CAB) issued a 'Show Cause Order,' directing IATA and other interested parties to demonstrate (show cause) why the antitrust immunity should not be withdrawn. Meanwhile, the CAB's tentative finding was that 'the Traffic Conference resolutions and related agreements are no longer in the public interest and should no longer be approved by the Board' (CAB, 1978).

By the end of February 1979, forty-six governments had made formal protests to the US Department of State in reaction to the Show Cause Order (SCO). IATA's comments to the CAB were accompanied by supportive submissions from forty-five airlines, five regional airlines associations, and two regional IGOs. Of the eleven other 'interested parties' submitting comments, seven supported IATA. Domestically, the US Department of Justice strongly supported the CAB's tentative decision to disapprove the IATA Traffic Conferences, whereas the Departments of State and Transportation urged moderation.

Faced with international and domestic opposition, the CAB gradually backed down. On 14 May 1979, it granted interim approval of the revised IATA provisions and terminated show cause proceedings on a long list of 'trade association' and 'facilitation' resolutions of IATA, while leaving open the issue of fare-related resolutions. On 30 August, the CAB further narrowed the scope of the SCO investigations to air travel directly affecting the United States, while granting continued antitrust immunity to traffic between non-US points. And a tentative CAB decision, issued on 15 April 1980 (CAB, 1980), barred participation by US airlines in IATA Traffic Conferences that coordinate rates for North Atlantic traffic between Europe and the United States, while granting two additional years of antitrust immunity to IATA rate-making elsewhere.

From early 1981 on, the center stage moved to intergovernmental forums. In February 1981, a tripartite meeting of the United States, Canada and ECAC (European Civil Aviation Conference) was convened in Washington. This was the first in a series of meetings searching for a compromise formula on North Atlantic fare-setting. In these negotiations, the Europeans pressed for further delays of the SCO in exchange for a potential tripartite agreement. A tentative agreement on a Memorandum of Understanding was worked out in late 1981 and finalized in May 1982. The accord granted antitrust immunity for North Atlantic tariff coordination within the IATA framework on the basis of a 'pricing zone' concept: carriers are free to raise or lower fares within certain limits without government approval.[1]

In many ways, the conflicts created by the US regime challenge were reminiscent of the confrontation between the forces of *laissez-faire* and regulation at Chicago in 1944. The American plea for 'deregulation' and free competition was stated primarily in terms of consumer benefits: increased competition will lead to lower fares. The domestic experiences of airline deregulation were frequently cited (see, e.g., Cohen, 1979). Most other states, however, argued in favor of continued regulation, emphasizing the differences between domestic and international aviation: international carriers operate in an environment where the principle of sovereignty reigns. Whereas unprofitable domestic carriers either merge or go out of business, they argued, neither option is available to prestigious national flagship carriers — instead, subsidy wars are likely to ensue. Finally, deregulation would lead to a redistribution of aircraft capacity away from the less and toward the more profitable routes, thinning out services to the Third World in particular, and aggravating the already serious congestion at popular destinations (see, e.g., Stainton, 1979).

The US challenge of the Chicago-Bermuda regime eventually resulted in changes within the regime rather than genuine regime change. *Rules* and *decision-making procedures* were modified. IATA made participation in the tariff coordination activities optional for its members, and the flexibility of fare-setting was increased. But the *principle* of international regulation as well as the *norms* of national claims on traffic and multilateralism survived. As a matter of fact, one ironic effect of US 'liberalization' and 'deregulation' efforts was growing government involvement in international aviation.

In sum, three different regime episodes have been identified in the history of international aviation, representing regime creation, change and persistence, respectively: the creation of the interwar 'unrestricted sovereignty' regime; the post-World War II revision, resulting in the 'Chicago-Bermuda' regime; and the less than successful attempt at regime change in the late 1970s and early 1980s. In the next chapter I shall explore structural and situational explanations of the observed regime episodes.

# 3 Explaining regime change in international aviation: A first cut

To what extent can the observed regime changes in international aviation be accounted for in terms of the models outlined in Chapter 1? That is the question which will be pursued in this chapter. It will be recalled that the models singled out for discussion focussed on technology, supply/demand dynamics, political structure and situational factors, respectively.

## Technology

Aviation, more than most issue-areas, is associated with technological innovation. Yet neither the major breakthroughs in propeller aircraft design in the 1930s (cf. Brooks, 1961: 67–84) nor the jet revolution of the early 1960s precipitated regime change.

The 1930s 'saw the realization in steel and aluminium of the previous decade's dreams' (Hildreth & Nalty, 1969: 195). In 1936 the Douglas DC-3 — 'the miracle passenger plane' (Becker, 1967: 218) — was introduced. Within three years, the DC-3 was carrying three of every four passengers flying on US airlines (Hildreth & Nalty, 1969: 206); and by 1946, 10,000 had been purchased by 174 airlines in seventy countries (Becker, 1967: 220). While representing a turning-point in commercial air transport, the development of large, long-range passenger planes in the 1930s did not entail any challenge to the existing aviation regimes.

To be sure, the introduction of original jets and, more recently, of jumbo jets led to intensified frictions between 'haves' and 'have-nots,' but once the new aircraft were integrated the industry seems to have been able to make the necessary adjustments without fundamental regime change (cf. Thornton, 1970: 44–5, 162–4). In the words of one observer:

If the international airline industry were other than one which involved all sorts of non-commercial and non-economic considerations the inevitable result of the economic conditions created by the jet revolution would have been a strong trend towards concentration. Small airlines would either have been squeezed out of business by bankruptcy or merged into larger units. In international air transport, however, this is unlikely to happen on any significant scale. Governments wish to preserve the separate identities of their own national airlines and would not allow them to be swallowed by large foreign airlines. (Wheatcroft, 1964: 108.)

In brief, technological factors do not seem to have been necessary, let alone sufficient, conditions of regime change in international air transport.

## Supply/demand dynamics

At the end of World War I a situation of 'surplus capacity' can be said to have existed in the leading countries of Western Europe. There was an abundance of surplus flying equipment, and thousands of airmen were looking for civilian work. However, the added supply was matched by increasing demand. Surface communications were generally poor as a result of the war. Governments were willing to give financial support to airline projects (cf. Davies, 1964: 10). Interestingly, international air transport, which would seem to be sensitive to fluctuations in the world economy, did not suffer any regime breakdown but instead showed continuous growth through the worst years of the depression of 1930–4 (Lissitzyn, 1942: 3).

Similarly, the surplus capacity in the wake of World War II was matched by a growing demand for civil air transport. As a by-product of the war, new and improved airfields had been built all over the world. At the same time, the travelling public was becoming increasingly air-minded (Davies, 1964: 239–40).

If it is thus hard to point to any supply/demand imbalance

which might have affected existing regimes in the early history of international aviation, surplus capacity did play a role in the attempted regime change in the 1970s. Some early signs began to appear in the mid-1960s. The precipitate acquisition of jets by all international airlines resulted in a huge increase in capacity, a reduction in growth rates, and financial losses. In late 1962 the IATA traffic conference unanimously agreed on a substantial fare increase aimed at solving financial problems. Whereas all European countries approved, the US CAB refused to accept the fare increase. The ensuing political crisis was finally solved in 1963 through joint government action. IATA and the European governments won this 'showdown at high noon with the U.S. government,' but at a heavy cost. The liberalization of charter rules and the unleashing of nonscheduled carriers in international markets can be seen as one American response to this defeat (Lowenfeld, 1975: 41).

The American nonscheduled airlines were built by wartime pilots immediately after World War II from the large stock of surplus military transport aircraft in the United States. Participation in the Berlin airlift and the Korean War gave the 'nonskeds' a strong claim to survival as a matter of national interest and made it possible to draw political support from the Defense Department and Congress. The US government came to pursue a policy of maintaining strong nonscheduled or 'supplemental' airlines as a reserve airlift capacity constantly ready to help out in military emergencies (Thayer, 1965: 90–112). By the mid-1960s the American military had developed an airlift capability of its own, and the supplementals were no longer considered essential for defense purposes (Thayer, 1965: 267).

Although the entrance of nonscheduled carriers into international aviation heralded surplus capacity, the economic boom and growth euphoria of the 1960s generally prevailed. The total ton kilometers performed by the scheduled airlines increased fourfold during the decade; the average international airfare decreased by almost 9 percent in current dollars; and the airlines were beginning to produce promising financial returns, 1966 being the year of peak profitability (Hammarskjöld, 1976). Growth was projected to continue at an even greater rate into the 1970s. Toward the end of the decade wide-bodied jets, which represented a doubling in seating capacity, were put into operation to meet the expected increase in demand.

As is well known, the world economy did not develop according to the optimistic extrapolations of the 1960s, and the airlines were hard hit by the economic recession, inflation, currency fluctuations and energy crises of the 1970s. First, air traffic demand did not match the increased capacity caused by the introduction of wide-bodied aircraft and the expanding international operations of supplemental carriers. American nonscheduled carriers were gaining an increasing share of the international market, especially on the North Atlantic. The free supplemental capacity in the wake of the gradual American disengagement in Southeast Asia contributed to this expansion. Concomitantly, the US charter rules became gradually liberalized, so that the operations of the supplementals were hardly distinguishable from those of regular airlines (Lipman, 1976: 7–8, 10–12). Sir Freddie Laker's Skytrain services, beginning in 1977, heralded the cave-in of the barrier between scheduled and charter operations on the European side of the Atlantic.

The inevitable result was unprecedented overcapacity on key routes, especially the critical North Atlantic routes. In 1975 unused capacity on the North Atlantic alone was equivalent to 15,000 empty Boeing 747 round trips (Hammarskjöld, 1977). The overcapacity problem was aggravated by rapidly increasing cost pressures. The impact of the energy crisis on airlines was particularly great. In just a few years the fuel share of total operating costs rocketed from 10 to 25 percent.

Since the existing regime did not allow predetermined capacity agreements, airlines turned to an incentive fares race to fill excess capacity and meet the low prices of charter competitors. The result was a swelling array of fares (excursion, inclusive tour, APEX, super-APEX, etc.) that created widespread confusion among carriers, travel agents, customers and government regulators alike, and made for large-scale 'cheating,' malpractice and intercarrier conflicts. As no major airline wanted to withdraw from the vital North Atlantic market, it turned into a source of universal financial losses.

In short, this surplus capacity no doubt contributed to the attempted regime change in the late 1970s. However, the proposed changes were not in the direction predicted by the model. The United States pressed for a more, rather than less, liberal regime.

## Political structure

Structural explanations of regime change, it will be recalled, may focus either on overall power structures or on issue-specific structures. Let us first consider the general model which rests on the assumption that since the strong make the rules, changes in the overall distribution of power — especially military power — entail regime changes. In view of the manifold civil-military interconnections in aviation, this model seems *a priori* applicable.

The airplane was first put to large-scale use in war. Military aircraft policy has largely dictated the types of vehicles available to the airlines, from 'stick-and-string' biplanes after World War I to today's supersonic jets (cf. Brooks, 1961: 141). National aviation policies have traditionally been formulated with a view to defense needs. Moreover, the norms guiding international aviation have been worked out in the wake of major wars. According to the overall structure model, wars tend to create regime change.

Legal opinion in most nations prior to World War I developed in favor of the principle of the freedom of the air. But between 1910 and the 1919 Paris conference, when airspace sovereignty was firmly established, war intervened, and 'when the Paris Convention was being drafted, aviation security questions, not commercial problems, were still uppermost in the minds of men' (Cooper, 1947: 129).

The prevalence of the 'realist' thinking associated with overall structural explanations goes a long way toward explaining the *contents* of the norms of the 1919 regime. Also, the establishment of the 'unrestricted sovereignty' regime can be said to have reflected the absence of a hegemon after World War I. The regime had an egalitarian taint. The sovereignty principle constituted a strong weapon of the weak in their interactions with the strong. Nor did the regime provide for any institutional arrangements which privileged the strong; instead, bilateral bargaining — where the 'power of the weak' could be exercised in full — was the predominant decision-making procedure. This could be accounted for by the change in overall structure as a result of the war. The period following World War I has been described as an 'interregnum between British dominance and American dominance in international economics and politics' when 'the former hegemonic power could no longer set the rules, and the rising hegemonic power had neither the will nor the power to assume this responsibility' (Gilpin, 1981: 234).

However, the direction of the subsequent regime *changes* is not readily accounted for by the overall structural model. First, the major changes in global politico-military power resulting from World War II were only imperfectly reflected in the aviation issue-area. The overall power structure emerging from the war was bipolar, with an unprecedented amassment of power in two superpowers, the United States and the Soviet Union. The postwar international aviation regime, in contrast, was characterized by the virtual absence of one superpower, the Soviet Union. From the birth of the Soviet state its priorities were focussed on domestic aviation, on solving the problem of the vast distances inside the Soviet Union. In the early postwar years the Soviet Union placed a very low priority on civil aviation in general. The Soviet Union, as noted above, did not participate in the Chicago conference, nor did it sign the Transit Agreement or join ICAO.

Second, the overall structure model cannot explain the less than successful attempts at regime change beginning in the late 1970s. The decline of American power, the Soviet achievement of strategic parity, and the emergence of China resulting in a 'triangular' great power structure are generally regarded as the most prominent shifts in the global politico-military distribution of power. In international aviation, however, American power remains unrivaled, and the US regime challenge was an attempt to capitalize on that power rather than a sign of American weakness. The Soviet Union, on the other hand, continues to stay largely outside the international aviation community, as does China. Not until the late 1950s were significant efforts made to develop a major civil air transport system in the Soviet Union (cf. Thornton, 1970: 9). While the Soviet carrier Aeroflot is today by far the largest domestic airline in the world, carrying as many passengers as the three biggest American domestic airlines combined, its international operations are still relatively modest and by the late 1970s ranked below those of Sabena, Aer Lingus or Saudi Arabian Airlines in terms of passengers carried (IATA, 1978). In 1970 the Soviet Union became a member of ICAO, but Aeroflot remains outside IATA. Nor has the Chinese airline, which is insignificant domestically as well as internationally, joined IATA, although in 1974 the People's Republic of China took the ICAO seat previously held by Taiwan.

Even a modified version of the overall structure model, which emphasizes economic rather than military hegemony, cannot adequately explain the observed regime changes in international aviation. The persistently strong position of Britain in the Chicago-Bermuda regime appears puzzling against the background of the rapidly disintegrating British empire. And why was the United States, rather than its economic challengers Japan and West Germany, pushing for regime change in the late 1970s? The hegemonic stability theory does not predict initiatives for regime change from a declining hegemon.

If we turn instead to issue structural explanations, power is assumed to be 'issue-specific' — the effectiveness of power bases may vary from issue-area to issue-area. What, then, are the determinants of national power specific to the international air transport issue-area?

A country's ability to generate traffic constitutes one power base. Countries may generate traffic in their capacity as terminal markets, that is by being either the source or the destination of travellers, or as transit markets (cf. Thornton, 1970: 49–60; Wassenbergh, 1970: 20). The geographical position of a country is of obvious importance. One asset is the possession of a large land mass that limits alternative international routes and enables a country to restrict the access of foreign carriers to a few gateway cities, thus preventing traffic to the hinterland except by national carriers. Power may also be derived from strategic operational locations necessary for refuelling, *en route* communication, navigational aids, and so on (Thornton, 1970: 61–71). Another issue-specific power base is the aeronautical 'know-how' and industry of a country.

No issue-specific power structure had crystallized by the end of World War I. No one country stood out as an undisputable aviation leader. However, the issue-structure model helps us understand the regime change in international aviation after World War II. The interwar period displayed a 'multipolar' or 'diffuse' issue structure. The center was in Europe. 'Because of the rivalry and competition among the Western European nations, as well as the limited range of early aircraft, air power first became of diplomatic and military importance in the European core of world politics' (Emme, 1959: 4). Germany emerged as a phoenix from the ashes of defeat in World War I to become one of the leading aviation nations. Denied a military air force but retaining political sovereignty over its airspace, Germany turned to a concentrated development of commercial air transport and technical advancement. By 1926 Germany's airlines carried more passengers, mail and cargo than all the other European nations combined (Emme, 1959: 9). Germany used its airlines to penetrate Latin America (Hall & Peck, 1941) and helped in the early establishment of civil air routes and supporting facilities in the Soviet Union (Kilmarx, 1962: 99). Its central geographical location and aeronautical know-how constituted principal German power bases.

Other aviation centers developed in the interwar years in the United States, Canada, Australia and the Soviet Union — all nations with vast territories — but since long-haul routes were not yet technically feasible, these countries concentrated their efforts on building domestic rather than international route networks. Their potential power remained largely unexploited internationally.

World War II resulted in a dramatic redistribution of issue-specific power in favor of the United States. Whereas the fleets and production capabilities of most other major aviation powers were seriously eroded as a result of the war, the United States had a fairly intact fleet and its production capacity was unscathed. In accordance with an understanding with Britain early in the war, the United States specialized in supplying the transport aircraft needs of the

Allies, whereas the British industry concentrated on the production of fighters and bombers. This understanding was tacit and informal, and its existence has later been questioned (see, e.g., Davies, 1964: 239). Yet in 1946 the British Permanent Secretary at the Ministry of Civil Aviation, Sir Henry Self, attributed the commanding lead of the United States in the sphere of transport aircraft to such an understanding (Cooper, 1947: 172).

Before the war, German and Italian airlines had extensive control or domination of air transport in South America. These operations were viewed as 'arteries of totalitarian propaganda, nerve centers of totalitarian espionage' (Hall & Peck, 1941: 347). Early in 1939 a series of interdepartmental conferences in Washington worked out a program to meet this challenge and expand US air services in Latin America. As none of the Axis countries would be permitted to retain their international routes or their aircraft production capability, the United States was uniquely poised to make the transition from military to commercial aviation.

Issue structuralism also accounts for Britain's strong position despite the overwhelming US superiority in aeronautical know-how and ability to generate traffic. Although the United States alone had the resources to operate worldwide immediately after World War II, it lacked route rights and landing rights for refuelling at bases located strategically along trunk routes. Hence Britain, by virtue of its extensive overseas colonies and Commonwealth connections, emerged as the chief countervailing power. At the same time, the bargaining strength of a number of otherwise insignificant countries possessing vital operating bases was enhanced. These included Iceland, Ireland and Portugal (the Azores). In short, Britain's issue-specific geographical assets in combination with the state of the technology in 1945 explain why the postwar international aviation regime did not turn into an American hegemony.

The recent challenge of the postwar regime can also be understood in terms of issue structuralism. United States aviation policy in the late 1970s was essentially an effort to exploit to the full its issue-specific power, which was constrained by the Chicago-Bermuda regime. Since 1945 the United States had retained and strengthened its leading position in aeronautical know-how and manufacture, often by perfecting and exploiting innovations made in other countries. Jet engines, for instance, owed their origin to work done in Britain. As a result of a series of accidents with early British jet transports, however, further development was delayed. Britain, as a consequence, lost its lead to American manufacturers who, by starting later, were able to take advantage of design features explored in the course of operating jet bombers (Brooks, 1961: 112–31; Wheatcroft, 1964: 92–4).

Furthermore, the United States remained the principal market for world air commerce, US domestic routes alone representing almost one-third of all air transport — domestic and international — in the world and involving more passengers than all international routes combined (Hammarskjöld, 1978b). Yet the American scheduled airlines were losing market shares internationally, especially on the vital North Atlantic routes. In 1950 Pan Am and TWA together carried 63 percent of the traffic on the North Atlantic, but by 1962 their combined share had shrunk to 36 percent (Corbett, 1965: 298). Similarly, the US dominance in aircraft manufacture proved to be a two-edged sword: as foreign airlines competing with American carriers on international routes have purchased the major share of their aircraft from American manufacturers, frequently with the help of Export-Import Bank loans, the US government has acquired a vested interest in the competitors of its own airlines. This has given foreign countries certain levers *vis-à-vis* the United States in bilateral negotiations (Thayer, 1965: 86–7. 281–2; Thornton, 1970: 104).

In sum, it was the underlying strength of the United States in the aviation issue-area, not American weakness or decline, that explained the attempted regime change. The United States tried to exploit its traffic-generating capacity to the full by pressing for free competition and by letting its powerful domestic airlines enter the international market.

## Situational explanations

The situation facing jurists, diplomats and militaries, as they began to worry about the international regulation of aviation in the early twentieth century, can be described as a dilemma. As the Dutch jurist Johanna Lycklama à Nijeholt (1910: 10) aptly summarized the first decade of legal discussions:

First, one is convinced that the sovereign state cannot be left without any authority over what happens just above its territory, and secondly, one shrinks from the idea that aerial navigation could be the object of narrow-minded restrictions. To bring these two ends together — the undeniable interest of the groundstate and sufficient freedom of intercourse for aerial navigation — proves to be the great difficulty and leads to the most different, and often strained solutions.

The horns of the dilemma were represented by military and commercial considerations, respectively. On the one hand, there was the fear of offensive actions by aircraft in warfare; on the other, the promise of air commerce. From the outset, a regime based on the principle of freedom of the air was considered to be the desirable cooperative solution, especially by jurists and in particular before international flights became a fact. The dilemma may be translated into a game matrix (Figure 3).

The situation resembles the game of prisoners' dilemma. To attain the mutually beneficial CC solution requires a considerable degree of mutual trust, since each party to an 'open-skies' regime may derive advantages at the expense of the others by defecting and closing its air boundaries.

There is ample evidence that the participating actors did, in effect, perceive the situation as such a dilemma. Analyzing British discussions in preparation for the peace conference in Paris after World War I, John Cooper (1947: 26) concludes:

Very obviously, British policy in 1918 looked in two directions: security of Great Britain in Europe required national control of the airspace over the homeland; future development of British international trade in the air, as farflung as British trade on the sea, and the desirability of the most rapid and adequate communication with the dominions and colonial empire, required minimum foreign

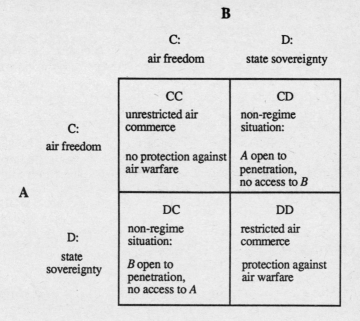

**Figure 3.** The international aviation dilemma in 1919

interference with British flight. From 1918 to this day British policy has faced this dilemma.

Whereas the early discussions among jurists centered around freedom of the air, the advent of World War I changed the calculus of payoffs. The cost of the CC solution rose dramatically, as a result of the demonstrable effects of air warfare. As the war came, states realized that they had too little to win and too much to risk by cooperating. Put differently, theoretical arguments and commercial interests were forced to take the back seat to military considerations; 'lessons of war and the need for security had proved that the safe answer as between sovereignty and freedom of the air was sovereignty' (Cooper, 1947: 22).

The freedom of the air versus airspace sovereignty debate was reopened as World War II was drawing to an end. But now the situation had become more ambiguous and complex. To be sure, in 1944 as in 1919, the costs of a CC solution based on air freedom had grown dramatically as a result of the devastation caused by air warfare. The principle of national airspace sovereignty had become firmly established. Yet in 1944 the lessons of war were tempered by experiences of aborted or delayed international routes because of non-cooperation in the 1930s. In other words, the costs of a DD solution had increased appreciably. The Canadian delegate at the Chicago conference, for instance, warned against 'a revival of the pre-war international rivalry in air transport' which 'would retard the development of efficient and economical air transport' (US Department of State, 1948: 74). A British White Paper of 1944 was quite explicit about the vices of the 1919 regime:

Summed up, the major evils of the pre-war period were, first, that any country on an international air route could hold operators of other countries to ransom even if those operators only wished to fly over or refuel in its territory; secondly, that there was no means of controlling the heavy subsidisation of airlines which all too often were maintained at great cost for reasons mainly of national prestige or as a war potential; and thirdly, that the bargaining for transit and commercial rights introduced extraneous considerations and gave rise to international jealousies and mistrust ... His Majesty's Government desire to see a radical change in this situation after the war. (UK Secretary of State for Air, 1944: 2.)

In addition, the number of flying nations had grown; the 1919 regime was drafted by an assembly of twelve states (the Aeronautical Commission of the Paris peace conference), whereas fifty-four states participated in the 1944 Chicago conference. And no longer could the problem facing the participants be construed as a simple either/or choice between air freedom and sovereignty. Subsumed under the main dilemma were at least two prominent 'sub-dilemmas.' On the one hand, the question had been raised whether international aviation should continue to be a national prerogative or be reorganized under an international authority. On the other hand, there was disagreement as to whether international air commerce should be subjected to regulation (by national governments or an international organization) or be left to the market forces and free competition (cf. Figure 4.)

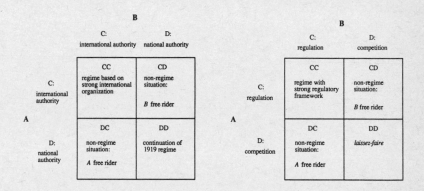

**Figure 4.** The international aviation dilemmas in 1944

Whereas the leading aviation powers — the United States and Britain — wanted to retain national control over international aviation, lesser powers called for its internationalization. New Zealand and Australia sought a far-reaching supranational arrangement in which a world organization would own and operate all international airlines, presumably under the aegis of the United Nations. Canada proposed an international authority to fix and allocate routes, frequencies, capacity and rates.

As for regulation versus competition, the Chicago conference witnessed the first — but by no means last — clash between two differing politico-economic traditions and philosophies, which had guided the evolution of civil aviation during the interwar years: on the one hand, the theory of 'regulated enterprise' prevalent in the United States, according to which government regulation aims at ensuring that private airlines are able to operate and compete freely with each other without disturbing the market function; on the other hand, the British (or rather European) notion of 'participatory enterprise' in which commerce in general is regarded as an instrument of national policy and airlines are owned in part or in full by governments (Lipman, 1976: 2).

The Chicago-Bermuda regime represents less of a clear-cut choice in a dilemma-like situation than did the unrestricted sovereignty regime of 1919. To be sure, the dilemma of national versus international control was resolved un-equivocally in favor of nationally owned airlines. But the emerging regime was a hybrid of competition-cum-regulation.

When the Chicago-Bermuda regime came under attack in the late 1970s, the clash was again between competition and regulation. The US 'deregulation' drive was premised on the perception that the costs of regime maintenance (CC) had increased, as far as the American carriers were concerned. They had lost market shares which could be recaptured under a more competitive regime. Even if other nations stuck to the Chicago-Bermuda regime, the US airlines were considered able to outcompete the IATA-regulated airlines in a price war. For most other aviation nations the payoff structure looked different. The gains of continued cooperation under the Chicago-Bermuda regime outweighed the uncertain prospects of a competitive regime. Even those countries in the Third World which were critical of the existing aviation order tended to be suspicious of the US challenge. In the words of one African airline representative:

in civil aviation we now find ourselves in a rather familiar confrontation similar to the North/South dialogue; we have the cards stacked against us in a very difficult game. And now some people want to change the rules so that the game becomes even more difficult. (Mathu, 1979: 2.)

The world of aviation had expanded dramatically since the Chicago conference. Now more than a hundred states had national airlines. In addition, several international organiza-tions — global as well as regional — were involved in aviation matters. What may have looked like a simple choice between regulation and deregulation (cf. Figure 5) was thus compli-cated by the multitude of interested actors.

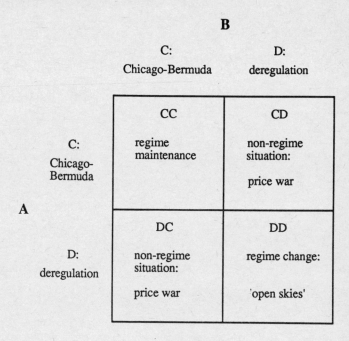

**Figure 5.** The international aviation dilemma in the late 1970s

A situational perspective on regime dynamics in the air transport issue-area reveals recurrent dilemmas facing aviation nations in their efforts at coordination and accommodation. The explanatory potency of situational factors seems greatest in the creation of the 1919 regime. The changed payoff structure as a result of World War I in combination with the relatively small number of involved actors clearly influenced the drafting of the Paris Convention.

Later regime change episodes cannot as readily be explained in situational terms. The situation after World War II represented less of a clearcut either/or choice, the payoff structure had not been unequivocally affected by lessons of the immediate past, and the number of actors had increased significantly. A situational analysis may contribute marginally to explaining why the US attempt at regime change in the late 1970s did not succeed by drawing attention to the fact that the United States acted upon a quite different payoff structure than most other aviation nations, and that the multitude of interested actors had become close to unmanageable.

# 4 Toward a process model of regime evolution

Economic, structural and situational explanations of regime creation and change are essentially *static*; they fail to take the dynamics of political *processes* into account. Even if this has been recognized by some students of international regimes, no coherent process model, comparable to the structural and situational models, has been developed. The purpose of this chapter is to outline precisely such a model, to be applied in subsequent chapters to the evolution of international aviation regimes. Let me preface my attempt by identifying different strands in the regime literature which seem to point in the direction of a possible process model.

## Embryos of a process model

Rejecting the 'mechanical metaphor' of structural models, Ernst Haas (1982: 241) concludes: 'What matters is process.' Others have echoed his call for greater attention to the dynamic, process-related aspects of regime evolution, albeit from different vantage points. One point of departure is the notion that different factors may explain regime formation, on the one hand, and regime maintenance or change, on the other. In the words of Charles Lipson (1982: 420), 'there may well be distinctive logics to regime initiation and regime maintenance.'

Several authors have commented on the relative autonomy of regimes and their resistance to change, once created:

A change in power distributions does not always imply a change in outcomes because regimes may function as intervening variables. Regimes may assume a life of their own, a life independent of the basic causal factors that led to their creation in the first place. (Krasner, 1982b: 499.)

This is so because 'the costs of regime maintenance are lower than those of establishing a new regime' (Lipson, 1982: 453). As noted by Machiavelli (1950: 21) almost five hundred years ago:

It must be considered that there is nothing more difficult to carry out, nor more doubtful of success, nor more dangerous to handle, than to initiate a new order of things. For the reformer has enemies in all those who profit by the old order, and only lukewarm defenders in all those who would profit by the new order, this lukewarmness arising partly from fear of their adversaries, who have the laws in their favour; and partly from the incredulity of mankind, who do not truly believe in anything new until they have had actual experience of it.

Machiavelli's idea that established institutional interests as well as human resistance to the new and unfamiliar stand in the way of new orders has been repeated by latter-day students of international regimes:

There are sunk costs involved in international institutions and thus they are not lightly to be changed or destroyed. The costs of reconstruction are likely to be much higher once regimes are consciously destroyed. Their very existence changes actors' incentives and opportunities. (Stein, 1982: 322–3.)
Social practices and convergent expectations frequently prove resistant to change, even when they produce outcomes that are widely understood to be undesirable or suboptimal. Existing institutional arrangements, such as the international agreements pertaining to coffee or Antarctica, are familiar constructs while new arrangements require actors to assimilate alternative procedures or patterns of behavior and to accept (initially) unknown outcomes. Additionally, planned changes in regimes require not only the destruction of existing institutions but also the coordination of expectations around new focal points. (Young, 1982: 280.)

This kind of logic has inspired the 'international organization model' suggested by Keohane and Nye (1977: 55), which is based on the assumption that:

a set of networks, norms, and institutions, once established, will be difficult either to eradicate or drastically to rearrange. Even governments with superior capabilities — overall or within the issue area — will find it hard to work their will when it conflicts with established patterns of behavior within existing networks and institutions. Under these conditions the predictions of overall structure or issue structure theories will be incorrect: regimes will not become congruent with underlying patterns of state capabilities, because international organizations as defined above will stand in the way.

The international organization model is described as 'much less deterministic than the basic structural models, leaving wide latitude for choice, decision, and multiple-level bargaining' (Keohane & Nye, 1977: 57). Essentially an explanation of why regimes do *not* change, it has not attracted the same wide attention as structural models among students of regime change. However, in a more recent book, Keohane (1984: 97) places the emphasis less on organizational inertia and more on the positive contributions of formal and informal organization:

Close ties among officials involved in managing international regimes increase the ability of governments to make mutually beneficial agreements, because intergovernmental relationships characterized by ongoing communication among working-level officials, informal as well as formal, are inherently more conducive to exchange of information than are traditional relationships between closed bureaucracies.

The role of *institutions* — 'defined broadly as sets of practices and expectations rather than in terms of formal organizations with imposing headquarters buildings' (Keohane, 1984: 246) — in providing *information* is thus key to Keohane's understanding of 'cooperation after hegemony.' As institutions, thus defined, prove their value in facilitating the exchange of information, demand for them increases (cf. Keohane, 1982: 348).

In more general terms, the international organization model along with Keohane's later refinement suggest that the *organizational context* of the multiple-level bargaining and exchange of information involved in the maintenance and reformation of regimes is a crucial parameter of a process model. Specifically, the existence or absence of transnational and transgovernmental links is singled out as a significant variable. Transnational links are 'interactions across state boundaries that are not controlled by the central foreign policy organs of governments' (Nye & Keohane, 1971a: xi); transgovernmental links refer to interactions between governmental sub-units across state boundaries (Nye & Keohane, 1971b: 383). Such links are assumed to facilitate the creation and maintenance of international regimes. According to Donald Puchala and Raymond Hopkins (1982: 247):

regime participants are most often bureaucratic units or individuals who operate as parts of the 'government' of an international subsystem by creating, enforcing or otherwise acting in compliance with norms. Individuals and bureaucratic roles are linked in international networks of activities and communication. These individuals and rules govern issue-areas by creating and maintaining regimes.

The reasoning thus far suggests that organization theory may provide elements of a process explanation of regime dynamics. However, the potentials of organization theory have not been explored fully by students of international regimes.

Although there has been little dialogue between students of complex organizations and students of international regimes, organization theory permits useful insights into the problem of international cooperation. Theorists in both fields have made strikingly similar observations: both recognize that the goals of potential collaborators are rarely unitary, and both make similar arguments about the importance of exchange of resources and information between the organization and its participants, to ensure the attainment of collective over individual goals. An overarching goal of collective action, noted by theorists in both fields, is the reduction of uncertainty. (Crawford & Lenway, 1985: 377.)

   In short, this perusal of existing fragments in the regime literature yields two main components of a process model of regime dynamics: (1) Bargaining and coalitions across and within state boundaries are essential in the formation, maintenance and change of international regimes. In other words, bargaining theory would seem to be of potential value in developing a process model. (2) The organizational context of bargaining and coalition-building is an important parameter. Hence, certain aspects of organization theory might be utilized. In addition, the distribution of information is considered a key element in the processes of regime dynamics; it is also an aspect which unites bargaining and organization theory.

## Bargaining and coalition-building

Situational models of regime change point to potential exchange situations, *bargaining situations*, as the foundations upon which regimes are built. These situations represent dilemmas for the involved actors. The 'bargaining problem' has been described as having three essential characteristics:

The first is that the two parties both realize that they could improve their lots if they made some sort of agreement — struck a bargain — with each other. ... The second characteristic is that mutual action is required to reach an agreement; there is no such thing as a unilateral bargain. ... The third feature of a bargaining problem is that there exists more than one possible agreement. (Pillar, 1983: 37.)

Bargaining *situations* frequently elicit bargaining *processes*, that is, processes of 'back-and-forth communication designed to reach an agreement when you and the other side have some interests that are shared and others that are opposed' (Fisher & Ury, 1983: xi). The outcome of a bargaining process is of course conditioned, but not determined, by the bargaining situation. Bargaining is more than automatic responses to particular situational stimuli. At the same time, one of the eternal paradoxes of bargaining is that 'it allows the weak to confront the strong and still come away with something which would not be possible if weakness and strength were all that mattered' (Zartman & Berman, 1982: 204). In other words, a bargaining perspective may yield additional insights not uncovered by either structural or situational models of regime dynamics.

A terminological clarification may be in order. Although frequently used interchangeably, the terms 'bargaining' and 'negotiation' may be kept apart. In my usage, 'negotiation' has a more narrow denotation than 'bargaining.' Negotiation refers to a formalized and explicit process of *verbal* exchange and represents but one aspect of bargaining. We may speak of a bargaining process even when the parties do not sit down at a negotiation table to exchange proposals; when communication is incomplete or indirect. Bargaining may, in fact be tacit, involving non-verbal acts, in which case 'adversaries watch and interpret each other's behavior, each aware that his own actions are being interpreted and anticipated, each acting with a view to the expectations that he creates' (Schelling, 1963: 21).

In other words, negotiation is a subcategory of bargaining which may be labelled explicit bargaining. Communication — 'any behavior, verbal or nonverbal, that is perceived by another person' (Johnson, 1974: 66) — is the key element of bargaining and negotiation.

Bargaining is one identifiable mode of social or joint decision-making, to be distinguished from majority decisions and judication. In majority decisions the choice is made by numerical aggregation, and in judication by a single authority who aggregates conflicting values and interests into a single decision. In bargaining, by contrast, the parties are left to themselves to combine their conflicting points of view into a single decision (Zartman, 1978: 69–70). Bargaining is the dominant mechanism of social choice among sovereign states which do not recognize any authority above and beyond themselves nor consider themselves bound by decisions to which they have not consented.

Although the transaction costs associated with bargaining are relatively high in international interactions, they are generally much lower than those associated with other available means of social choice, such as coercive diplomacy or organized warfare. In other words, 'the prominence of bargaining as a mechanism of social choice in the international policy stems from its *relative* efficiency rather than from any claim to efficiency in *absolute* terms' (Young, 1978: 251). The prominence of bargaining, in turn, means that most international regimes are 'negotiated orders' rather than 'spontaneous' or 'imposed' orders, to use Oran Young's (1982: 282–5) terminology.

Whereas the static game-theoretical conception of bargaining *situations* is based on the assumption of individual rational choice, bargaining *processes* are better understood in terms of 'the logic of cybernetics' (cf. Steinbruner, 1974: 14):

In essence, it is cognitive operations of the human mind working in interaction with the organizational structure of the government which set workable limits on highly diffuse decision problems, and it is cybernetic theory, thus supplemented, which offers a base paradigm for political analysis competitive with the rational position.

A cybernetic model regards bargaining as a 'self-stabilizing (i.e., outcome-reaching) process of output and feedback' and the bargaining actors as 'a pair of linked servomechanisms' (Zartman, 1976: 37). Trial-and-error search, information processing and uncertainty control are basic elements of the cybernetic understanding of bargaining. Uncertainty, rather than the game-theoretical notion of complete information, is the fundamental assumption of the cybernetic model. The bargaining process can be seen as 'a learning process in which each party is both teacher and student' (Zartman & Berman, 1982: 19), but it is a 'constrained learning process' insofar as the teachers-cum-students will process information in such a way that conceptual change will be kept within reasonably narrow limits (Steinbruner, 1974: 330).

From the viewpoint of game theory, bargaining can be seen as communication superimposed on a game. The human capacity to acquire, reveal and conceal information then becomes crucial, and creates the problem of interpretation associated with communicative acts. This reconceptualization puts cognition at center stage. The problems raised by selective attention and interpretation, rather than being shunned as in game theory, become analytical points of departure. The logic of cybernetics in combination with cognitive theory suggest a model which regards information processing as the link between interstate bargaining and decision-making within the state, and which views bargaining as a process of adjusting initial expectations and interpretations (cf. Jönsson, 1983).

At the outset, each bargaining actor has a set of *expectations* about how the adversary is likely to act and respond to his own moves. In the course of the bargaining process each actor is able to test and either validate or adjust his initial expectations. The decisional output from one of the actors serves as informational input into the other actor's decision-making process.

Expectations and interpretations are affected to a considerable extent by the actors' *belief systems*, built up as a result of their past experiences. These belief systems complicate the mutual adjustment process that has to occur, if bargaining is to usher in an agreement. First, *incompatible beliefs* among the bargaining actors frequently complicate and aggravate international bargaining. They open up the possibility of *misperception*: the message sent by actor *A* need not be the message received by actor *B*. Moreover, all research on cognitive processes indicates that belief systems are *resistant to change* (see, e.g., Jervis, 1976: 291–6).

A fundamental *credibility* problem adheres to all verbal and non-verbal communication in bargaining processes. Deception is a manifest possibility in bargaining and negotiations. From the viewpoint of the sender, it is a matter of how to communicate resolve — how to incur commitments — convincingly. For the receiver, the question is how to determine whether the adversary signals what he means and means what he signals.

From the viewpoint of the involved parties, a bargaining process may appear as a series of dilemmas or 'tightropes' (Rubin, 1983: 136–7) rather than a process of rational problem-solving. Subsumed under the basic dilemma of cooperation versus competition, epitomized by the prisoners' dilemma metaphor, are a number of sub-dilemmas: honesty versus misrepresentation, clarity versus vagueness, gain in the long run versus short-term gain, bundling versus breaking down issues, etc. These choices represent genuine dilemmas, insofar as no optimal solution exists. The actors often resort to middle-of-the-road solutions or 'balancing acts' of the type 'cooperative egotism' (Weiss-Wik, 1983: 722), 'firm flexibility' (Pruitt, 1983: 169), and so on.

In contrast to the rationality model, according to which each actor performs a comprehensive search and a detailed evaluation of all available alternatives, the cybernetic paradigm suggests that 'the central focus of the decision process is the business of eliminating the variety inherent in any significant decision problem' (Steinbruner, 1974: 56). In a bargaining context, this implies searching for a *formula*, 'a shared perception or definition of the conflict that establishes terms of trade' (Zartman & Berman, 1982: 95). One implication of viewing negotiation as a process for eliminating variety and reducing uncertainty is that 'the development of common perceptions becomes more important than the exchange of concessions' (Winham, 1977: 97). Applied to negotiations about an international regime, the search for a formula, if successful, will establish the principles and norms of the regime.

Unlike situational explanations of regime creation and change, which regard regimes as responses to specific, well-defined situations, a bargaining perspective recognizes that broadening the scope of discussions beyond the immediate situation is a common negotiating tactic. *Issue linkage* represents an attempt to exploit one's relative issue-specific power in an extraneous issue-area to compensate for one's weakness in the issue-area that is the subject of negotiations. Issue linkage can be mutually beneficial and can facilitate agreements that might not otherwise be possible, but may also complicate cooperation — especially if it takes the form of 'blackmailing' rather than 'backscratching' (Axelrod & Keohane, 1985: 239–40).

Moreover, international negotiations require agreements not only across the table but also on each side of the table. In fact, international negotiations have been characterized as 'about 90 percent negotiation with one's compatriots' (Zartman & Berman, 1982: 207; cf. Winham, 1979: 116). The fact that internal bargaining processes run parallel to international negotiations places each negotiator in a 'boundary-role' position (Druckman, 1978). Having to bargain horizontally (with the other side) as well as vertically (with his constituents), the negotiator often experiences dilemmas.

The drive to appear competent to a constituency results in a dilemma for negotiators. In many cases, the behaviors that are necessary for creating the conditions conducive to a negotiated contract may be the same behaviors that make the negotiator appear incompetent to his or her constituency. In order to reach any compromise, concessions are necessary. However, concessions can easily be interpreted by the constituency as a sign of weakness. Creating firm public stands on positions may be counterproductive in the creation of a problem-solving atmosphere for negotiation. Yet, such public stands are critical for the development of constituency support. (Neale & Bazerman, 1985: 37–8.)

Just as situational models assume that an increasing number of actors makes cooperation more difficult, as we have seen in Chapter 1, so multilateral negotiations are generally considered more difficult and less likely to reach comprehensive agreements than bilateral ones. In negotiations with many participating actors more values, interests and perceptions have to be integrated or accommodated, and there is more uncertainty as to the interests and motives of other participants. It is therefore harder to find a solution acceptable to everyone. There is a strong likelihood that multilateral negotiations will produce only 'partial' solutions, in terms of covering only some of the agenda items, leaving some disagreement latent in ambiguous wording, or being signed by only some of the negotiating parties (cf. Midgaard & Underdal, 1977: 332–9).

To that extent, the conclusions of situational theories are underpinned by a bargaining perspective. However, while making comprehensive cooperative solutions more difficult, bargaining among a multitude of actors also gives rise to 'the forming of subgroups and of unofficial channels of communication' (Midgaard & Underdal, 1977: 337). *Mediation* and *coalition-building* are well-known ways of overcoming the negative effects of multilateral and multiple-level bargaining. Coalitions may be built between, within and across nations. Those interested in, as well as those opposed to, an agreement may form national and transnational coalitions. Thus, international regimes often rest on a coalition of 'winners' and may have to face the opposition of a coalition of 'losers.'

In summary, a bargaining perspective on regime dynamics directs our attention to a process in which uncertainty and 'constrained learning' play major roles. Does bargaining make a difference? To what extent may a bargaining perspective yield conclusions that do not follow from structural or situational models? First, the bargaining perspective outlined above does not treat states as unitary actors. The search for a 'formula' in terms amenable to an agreement involves the formation of coalitions within and across nations as well as mediation and brokerage by informal subgroups.

Second, the bargaining perspective may explain why a regime is *not* created or changed, although structural and situational models predict such adjustments. The mutual adjustments that are necessary in order to reach an agreement on the creation or revision of a regime may be impeded by the belief systems of the involved actors; beliefs may be incompatible and are resistant to change; misperceptions may act as obstacles to agreement.

Third, the linkage of issues in the bargaining process may 'contaminate' the effect of issue-specific structural or situational factors and either facilitate or aggravate the attainment of regime agreements. As noted by Axelrod and Keohane (1985: 239, 240), 'linkage can be beneficial to both sides in a negotiation, and can facilitate agreements that might not otherwise be possible'; yet 'not all issue-linkages promote agreement, any more than each exercise of power can be expected to lead to cooperation.' To the extent that issues are linked through 'blackmailing' (threats) rather than 'backscratching' (promises), regime agreements are less likely to occur.

Fourth, the bargaining perspective directs our attention to the fact that a regime is generally the result of a *compromise* rather than a direct, rational response to structural or situational factors. The creation of a regime is not necessarily an either/or choice; through cross-cutting coalitions, issue-linkage and other negotiating tactics, the involved actors try to find some middle ground between opposing standpoints.

The bargaining relationship poses a series of dilemmas for the involved actors and puts the negotiators in problematic 'boundary roles.' As pointed out earlier, the organizational context of the multiple-level bargaining process is of particular importance. Let us therefore now turn to a consideration of how organization theory may supplement the bargaining perspective outlined above.

## Organizational context

It will be recalled that several authors have pointed to the significance of international and transnational organizations in the evolution of regimes. It has also been suggested that organization theory may provide largely overlooked insights into regime dynamics. Thus, the study of organization generally and international organization (IO) in particular should contain clues of relevance to a process model of regime dynamics.

First, it should be noted that the relation between general organization theory and IO studies has largely been one of mutual neglect. Widely used textbooks on organization theory, though aspiring to 'summarize and report the present state of knowledge about human organizations' (March, 1965: ix), include no systematic treatment of international organizations (Cf., e.g., March, 1965; Nystrom & Starbuck, 1981). Nor do the authors of textbooks on international organizations make use of general organization theory (Cf., e.g., Claude, 1964; Jacobson, 1979).

The few analysts who do address the possible applicability of organization theory to IO studies normally reach negative conclusions (cf. e.g., Haas, 1964; Gordenker & Saunders, 1978). However, the proliferation of organizations nationally as well as internationally in our century raises the generic problem of interorganizational relations. I agree with Leon Gordenker and Paul Saunders (1978) that, among the variety of organization theories, those which focus on the relationship of organizations to their environment — especially to other organizations — seem most relevant to students of international organization.

Some significant steps have been taken in that direction. Frederick Thayer (1981) makes a normatively tinted plea for 'structured non-hierarchy.' He points out that the notion that formal organizations have ambiguous and fluid boundaries and tend to penetrate and permeate each other is akin to John Herz's (1959) idea of the increased 'permeability' of one type of formal organization, the nation-state. Rejecting the traditional, antipodal command and market models, Thayer submits as an ideal design for international organization a model of non-hierarchical 'overlapping groups' at various levels with some individuals designated as 'linking-pins' who act as communication channels through which consensus may be reached.

In a more empirically orientated paper, Andrew Scott (1981) suggests the applicability of an information perspective to relationships between international organizations and their environments. He finds the concept of 'informal organization' a valuable one for the study of IO and argues that informal networks will increase in importance as instruments for coordination and coalescence, as the total number of transnational organizations continues to grow. Anthony Judge (1978) shares Scott's preference for network analysis and explores relevant network theory in some detail.

Nonetheless, the recent interest among organization theorists in interorganizational relations has had no immediate repercussions in studies of IO or of international regimes. Students of IO, like organization theorists, have traditionally been concerned chiefly with intra-organizational phenomena. Even Scott, who favors an approach focussing on the interface between international organizations and their environment, fails to recognize the contributions by inter-organization theorists while lamenting the shortcomings of micro-orientated organization theory (Scott, 1981: 17–18).

While indeed 'most organizational research explicitly or implicitly assumes that organizations can be sharply distinguished,' the realization has gained ground that 'often, it is unclear where organizations end and environment begins' (Metcalfe, 1981: 505). Among organization theorists this realization has been gradual. First, the conventional 'closed-system' analysis of self-contained organizational units gave way to an 'open-system' perspective, emphasizing the influence of the external environment on individual organizations (see, e.g., Thompson, 1967). A second step was to choose interaction between different organizations as the unit of analysis and try to identify relevant 'organization-sets' (see, e.g., Aldrich & Whetten, 1981). A more recent refinement has been the focus on 'informal organization' rather than formal relations of authority within and between units (see, e.g., Bacharach & Lawler, 1980). In interorganization theory this has entailed growing interest in varieties of *network analysis.*

A social network may be loosely defined as 'a patterned set of relationships among actors or groups in a social space' (Bacharach & Lawler, 1980: 205) or a 'structure of recurrent transactions' (Aldrich, 1982: 282). Networks are constructs created by researchers to guide analysis. Thus 'inter-organizational networks are identified by tracking down all of the ties binding organizations in a population defined and explicitly bounded by an investigator' (Aldrich, 1979: 324).

Effective international regimes are often associated with the existence of transnational networks and concomitant informal contacts and communication among organizations and officials. As we have seen, this is suggested as a major reason why the creation of regimes, on the one hand, and regime maintenance and change, on the other, may have different explanations.

Governments no longer act within such regimes as unitary, self-contained actors. 'Transgovernmental' networks of acquaintance and friendship develop, with the consequences that supposedly confidential internal documents of one government may be seen by officials of another; informal coalitions of like-minded officials develop to achieve common purposes; and critical discussions by professionals probe the assumptions and assertions of state policies. These transgovernmental relationships increase opportunities for cooperation in world politics by providing policy makers with high-quality information about what their counterparts are likely to do. Insofar as they are valued by policy makers, they help to generate demand for international regimes. (Keohane, 1982: 349.)

In short, the existence or absence of transnational networks within an issue-area obviously makes a difference for the bargaining process leading to the initiation or revision of an international regime. To understand why this is so, let us look closer at what kind of actors and relationships are assumed to make up transnational networks of relevance to the evolution of regimes.

National organizational networks typically include both

private and public organizations and therefore have to operate concurrently in markets and hierarchies. In other words, network analysis encompasses entities which normally are studied in terms of separate analytical frameworks (Hjern & Potter, 1981; Hernes, 1978). This applies, *a fortiori*, to transnational organizational networks where national networks of private and public organizations constitute subsystems and intergovernmental (IGOs) as well as nongovernmental (NGOs) international organizations typically participate.

The notion that networks are composed of diverse organizations needs to be qualified. Participants in networks are not organizations in their entirety but rather certain role occupants in the constituent organizations.

> We should not forget that organizations, as such, do not interact with the environment. Individuals do the interacting, and they do it within a greater or less detailed framework of role demands, role expectations, role conflicts, and resultant role stress. (Organ, 1971: 80.)

The interface between organizations consists primarily of 'boundary-role' occupants, linking an organization to its environment through either information processing or external representation (Roos & Starke, 1981: 302). As noted above, negotiators for organizations are boundary-role occupants; and as suggested then, boundary-role occupants are typically susceptible to a high degree of role conflict. They frequently get caught in the crossfire between divergent role expectations, not only between those of their own organization and other organizations, but also between varying role conceptions among their own constituents.

As 'activist brokers' between their own organization and its environment, boundary-role occupants must not only represent the organization to its environment, but also represent the environment to their constituents. They are therefore apt to feel more keenly than their constituents the defects in their organization and to become agents of organizational change. In their interaction with outsiders, boundary-role occupants can rarely base their influence on formal authority but have to rely on more subtle means of influence, such as expertise and personal friendship (Organ, 1971: 74–6).

Boundary-role occupants may be found at various levels of national organizational structures. In international organizations they are typically found within the secretariat. National and international boundary-role occupants alike are predominantly bureaucrats. The bureaucratization of decision-making in international organizations has been noted (Cox & Jacobson, 1973: 424–5). Harold Jacobson's (1979: 141) characterization of international organizations as 'meta-bureaucracies' applies all the more to transnational networks. Boundary roles do not necessarily follow formal positions, and boundary-role occupants constitute only fractions of national administrative units and international secretariats.

Students of interorganizational networks have pointed to the centrality of so-called *linking-pin organizations* in such networks.

Linking-pin organizations that have extensive and overlapping ties to different parts of a network play the key role in integrating a population of organizations. Having ties to more than one action-set or subsystem, linking-pin organizations are the nodes through which a network is loosely joined. (Aldrich & Whetten, 1981: 390.)

Interorganizational networks are often represented in the form of graphs, using points (or nodes) as symbols of organizations (or, more correctly, boundary roles in organizations) and arrows as symbols of relations (with the head of the arrows indicating the directionality of relations). Figure 6 offers a hypothetical example.

In such graphic representations, linking-pin organizations occupy central positions in terms of being reachable from, and able to reach, most other organizations in the network (such as organization 10 in our hypothetical example). Thus, linking-pin organizations may serve as communication channels between organizations in the network, may link third parties to one another, and may actively direct the behavior of other organizations or coalitions (cf. Aldrich & Whetten, 1981: 390; Tichy, 1981: 229). In short, linking-pin organizations tend to occupy broker roles in networks (Aldrich, 1982: 288–91).

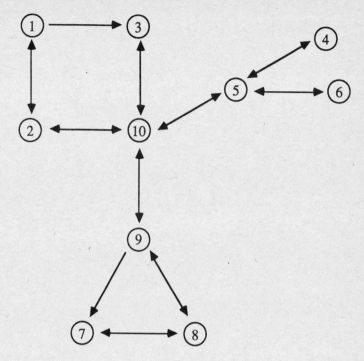

**Figure 6.** Graphic representation of network links

The position of a linking-pin organization is seldom based entirely on formal authority but rests in large measure on its ability to manipulate network characteristics by mobilizing coalitions around specific issues or controlling the bargaining process (Aldrich & Whetten, 1981: 394). Linking-pin organizations thus seem to face the same dilemma as 'unauthorized mediators' in international negotiations. Their ability to serve as impartial brokers is often complicated by their obvious self-interest in the issues under deliberation, making other actors uncertain whether their interests are being mediated or manipulated (cf. Stenelo, 1972: 37–43).

Within a given issue-area it is possible — at least theoretically — to identify a set of organizations which tend to become involved in the preparation, making and implementation of decisions within that issue-area and which maintain direct or indirect links with each other. We might refer to this set of organizations as a *potential* network. That part of the potential network which becomes operative in the handling of a specific issue might be labelled a *mobilized* network.

How, then, does all this relate to the bargaining perspective outlined earlier in this chapter? First, *communication* is the basic content of interorganizational relations within a network (Aldrich & Whetten, 1981: 385). Second, *bargaining* and *coalition* between participant organizations are prevalent processes in transnational networks. Samuel Bacharach and Edward Lawler's (1980) depiction of individual organizations as political bargaining systems applies *a fortiori* to transnational organizational networks which normally consist of formally autonomous organizations with diffuse accountability and division of responsibility rather than hierarchically ordered entities with fixed accountability (cf. Sharkansky, 1981: 462). Third, both bargaining theory and network analysis point to boundary-role occupants as key actors in horizontal and vertical bargaining.

Finally, a network approach underlines and reinforces the bargaining perspective's treatment of states as less than unitary actors. On the one hand, the existence of a transnational network presumably facilitates the building of those coalitions and compromises which are needed for the creation or revision of international regimes. Linking-pin organizations may act as brokers. By probing not only the current positions of the involved parties but also their flexibility, linking-pin organizations may simplify the formation of international consensus (cf. Figure 7).

On the other hand, a transnational network — to the extent that it owes its existence to, and has a stake in, a specific regime — may fortify the existing regime and render regime change more difficult. It will be recalled that this was the underlying notion of Keohane and Nye's (1977) original 'international organization model' of regime change.

To summarize, the process model proposed in this chapter combines insights from bargaining theory and inter-organization theory. Bargaining intervenes between the dilemma-like situation facing the actors and the creation or transformation of an international regime. The existence of transnational networks is of crucial importance in such multiple-level bargaining. Networks facilitate the distribution

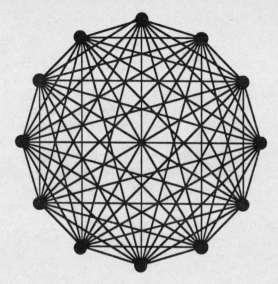

12 states in a multilateral bargaining
situation without a 'broker'

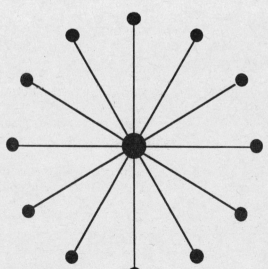

but is the broker a
rep of a hegemon?.

12 states in a bargaining situation
with an IGO acting as a "broker"

**Figure 7.** Interaction patterns among twelve states

of information, which is considered a key element in the process of regime dynamics, and are instrumental in building coalitions and mediating divergent interests. Networks rest on interorganizational links through individuals in boundary-role positions.

The resulting perspective may remind political scientists of Graham Allison's (1971) Model III, or 'bureaucratic politics' model, writ large. That model presumes no unitary actor but rather many bureaucratic actors as players — actors who tend to see different faces of the issue at hand. To explain a particular decision — in Allison's case national foreign policy decisions, in our case international decisions to create, maintain, or transform regimes — 'it is necessary to identify the games and players, to display the coalitions, bargains, and compromises, and to convey some feel for the confusion' (Allison, 1971: 146).

Allison's model views international relations as the overlap of intra-national games:

The actions of one nation affect those of another to the degree that they result in advantages and disadvantages for players in the second nation. Thus players in one nation who aim to achieve some international objective must attempt to achieve outcomes in their intra-national game that add to the advantages of players in the second country who advocate an analogous objective. (Allison, 1971: 178.)

In the perspective outlined above, however, 'bureaucratic politics' does not stop at the water's edge. There may, in fact, exist cross-national links in the form of informal networks in which bureaucrats — national and international — play key roles.

# 5 Negotiating the first aviation regime

The first forums, in which the idea of an international regime for air transport was broached, were assemblies of jurists. As early as 1880 the Institute of International Law, 'a private association of eminent jurists from nearly every civilized country' (Colegrove, 1930: 42), included the subject of aviation in a draft convention on the laws of war. In 1900 the French publicist Paul Fauchille proposed that the Institute direct its attention to a code of laws to regulate aerial navigation in peacetime as well as war. In the following year Fauchille published his epoch-making study *Domaine aérien et le régime juridique des aérostats*, and at the 1902 session of the Institute he presented a draft code of international law based on the concept of freedom of the air (Kuhn, 1910: 111; Richards, 1912: 18; Colegrove, 1930: 42).

At a later meeting of the Institute in 1906, Fauchille's doctrine was challenged by the British law professor John Westlake, who proffered a resolution on the basis of state sovereignty over the airspace above its territory. A majority of 14 to 9 voted in favor of Fauchille's resolution (Colegrove, 1930: 42; Cooper, 1947: 18). Thus, the agenda was set and the lines of demarcation were drawn several years before the first aircraft crossed national boundaries.

The earliest discussions therefore had a rather theoretical and abstract character. 'Where precedent fails, analogy gives the clue and accordingly the great fluid of atmosphere surrounding the world has been likened to the high seas, with the sole difference that the sea of air abuts upon the sovereignty beneath in a vertical instead of horizontal direction' (Kuhn, 1910: 112). Hence advocates of air freedom and defenders of state sovereignty alike drew heavily on existing international and national laws, especially the law of the sea.

Those jurists who argued in favor of air freedom referred to the principle of the freedom of the seas, first expounded by Hugo Grotius in the early seventeenth century. Like the *mare liberum* doctrine, the notion of air freedom was predicated on the impossibility of effective control by any state (cf. Kuhn, 1910: 112–13). Proponents of state sovereignty, on the other hand, questioned the air-sea analogy. Activities in the airspace above a state were considered far more dangerous to the state than activities in the adjoining sea; hence, 'as long as the law of gravity prevails, a State must have unfettered control over air vessels passing above its territories, in order to protect itself and to carry on its administration' (Richards, 1912: 8). The preferred analogy was rather prevalent municipal law, which recognized private ownership of property 'to the center of the earth' to cover mining. That principle was seen to imply private ownership and, by extension, state sovereignty in the air *usque ad coelum* (Richards, 1912: 12–13).

The analogy with territorial waters was made by certain adherents of both air freedom and state sovereignty. Just as state sovereignty had been extended beyond the territory to adjacent waters, so a lower zone of territorial airspace might be established. And just as the sea beyond the territorial waters was free, so one could conceive of a higher zone of free airspace above a certain agreed altitude. Different suggestions were made as to where to draw the borderline between territorial and free airspace. A common principle was that the territorial zone should reach as high as the state could exercise its authority. In the case of territorial waters, borders were originally determined by the range of cannons; the territorial airspace might, by analogy, extend as far as the range of artillery. Fauchille, for example, suggested 1,500 meters as the limit. Other proposals recognized sovereignty to an unlimited altitude, but restricted by the right of 'innocent passage' (another concept borrowed from the law of the sea) for air traffic (cf. Lycklama à Nijeholt, 1910: 11–14).

In short, the cleavage between the advocates of air freedom and state sovereignty was not as irreconcilable as the situational model suggests. There was indeed room for compromise. What was at issue was essentially whether the freedom of passage was to be regarded as a right (air freedom) or a concession (state sovereignty) (Lycklama à Nijeholt, 1910: 15).

Moreover, the early discussions among jurists in the Institute of International Law and other forums seem to have created an embryonic transnational network with potential influence on subsequent negotiations. At the 1910 Paris conference several of the delegates were members of this network of jurists. Paul Fauchille, for instance, played a prominent role in the French delegation.

The 1910 conference, however, also marked the end of the predominance of jurists in the deliberations of an international aviation regime. The delegations of the smaller European states consisted of diplomatic personnel, whereas the greater powers sent military men along with lawyers and diplomats. Some delegations — such as the British, Russian and Spanish — were indeed dominated by military professionals (Conférence internationale, 1910: 3–7).

The French government had carefully planned the 1910 conference. An interministerial commission had prepared a questionnaire to serve as a basis for discussions at the conference. In August 1909 this questionnaire was circulated to the participating states, who were asked to submit their preliminary official views on the suggested agenda items. The conference program was rather narrow and technical in scope. Between December 1908, when the French government sent invitations to the conference, and August 1909 France had apparently decided to avoid discussion of the fundamental question of air freedom versus state sovereignty (Cooper, 1968: 107).

The French cited two principal reasons for this attempt to narrow the agenda. First, a broader scope would jeopardize the success of the conference. The two principles were too far apart to hope for a common formula (*formule d'accord*); furthermore, it was a theoretical issue of 'juridical metaphysics' which ought to be discussed among law professors rather than diplomats. The second motive was that, in practice, the divergence was not considered to be of great consequence; regardless of which principle they adhered to, the delegates ought to be able to agree on many practical matters of air transport (Conférence internationale, 1910: 242).

The French effort to limit the scope did not succeed. The replies of some governments to the French questionnaire forced a broadening of the conference agenda. The Germans replied with a complete draft for an international convention of forty-three articles and two annexes, 'the first multilateral air navigation convention ever prepared,' as well as 'the first concrete statement by a sovereign State of its position on the legal status of flight-space' (Cooper, 1968: 108, 110). The German proposal did not challenge airspace sovereignty directly, but was construed by the British as authorizing freedom of the air (Cooper, 1947: 19). The ambiguity of the German position was accentuated by additional statements at the Paris conference which seemed to favor general freedom of flight (Cooper, 1968: 111).

The position of the French government was based on Paul Fauchille's notion of air freedom, tempered by the self-preservation rights of subjacent states (Cooper, 1968: 109). The discussions at the 1910 conference centered around the German and the French proposals. The chairman of the French delegation, Louis Renault, a distinguished international lawyer and a member of the Institute of International Law, presided over the conference. And the equally renowned judge Dr Kriege, head of the German delegation, presided over its important First Committee, in which the rival principles of air freedom and state sovereignty were debated under an agenda item verbosely entitled 'Examination of the Principle of Admission of Air Navigation within the Limits of or above Foreign Territory; that is to say, Belonging to a State Other Than That from Which the Aircraft Comes' (Colegrove, 1930: 48; Cooper, 1968: 108).

The German and French proposals were opposed chiefly by the British delegation, chaired by Admiral Douglas Gamble. In its reply to the French questionnaire, the British government had made it clear that it considered it 'desirable that no regulation be instituted which implies in any manner whatsoever the right of an aircraft to fly over or land on private property, or which excludes or limits the right of every State to prescribe the conditions under which one may navigate in the air above its territory' (Cooper, 1968: 112). At the conference table in Paris, the British delegation consistently and unequivocally upheld the principle of state

*Was the British position a response to the threat of air transport or a challenge to sea transport which would threaten the British traditional realm.*

sovereignty and argued that every state, as a matter of 'international courtesy', might arrange reasonable facilities for foreign aircraft to fly above, or land in, its territory. The security aspects of air transportation were emphasized by the British (Conférence internationale, 1910: 269–72).

In short, the 1910 conference in Paris revealed differences not only between different European countries but also between legal and military points of view. Though less visible, there were divergences within the participating states, in addition to interstate disagreements. As John Cooper (1947: 19) has noted, 'the jurists heading the French delegation seemed to agree with the German position on legal grounds, although there is reason to believe that the French military and naval delegates were very doubtful of the advisability of the French position.' The German delegation also included military representatives as well as lawyers, and the ambiguity of the German position at the conference may well have reflected internal differences. The British delegation was more homogeneous, reflecting the views of the Admiralty and War Office who 'were persistently opposed to any limitation upon the right of a state to close its air space to the entrance of the aircraft of any or all nations' (Colegrove, 1930: 50).

The jurists seemingly prevailed at the Paris conference. General agreement was reached on a draft convention of fifty-five articles and three annexes covering such matters as nationality and registration of aircraft, certificates of navigability, and rules for departure and landing. One observer estimates that 'had a majority rule been in effect at the Paris conference in 1910 and had a vote been taken, a convention might then have been adopted on this majority vote solemnly recognizing as the long-established Law of Nations that the "air is free"' (Cooper, 1947: 33). Yet, on 29 June, upon the motion of the British, the conference adjourned *sine die* without the signing of a treaty. The ostensible reason for the British move was that the extreme importance of the questions covered by the draft convention necessitated government consideration before approval was given (Conférence internationale, 1910: 62).

Subsequent parleys between governments to find a way out of the *impasse* proved fruitless. The first intergovernmental discussions thus failed to produce an international regime. Kenneth Colegrove's (1930: 51) epitaph is worth noting:

In one sense, the conference of 1910 marks the end of the first phase of the development of international regulation of aviation. The hasty attempt to secure an international declaration for complete freedom of the air before unfavorable national legislation had time to crystallize proved to be a failure. Perhaps it would have been unwise to circumvent national prejudices in this fashion, and perhaps the convention, if signed and ratified, would have been more honored in the breach than in the observance. At any rate, the insistence of the originators of the conference upon a declaration of freedom of aerial circulation and the resistance of the British to such a declaration blocked the opportunity to secure at that time an international convention which included many rules upon which there was general agreement.

To be sure, jurists continued to debate air freedom. At the 1911 session of the Institute of International Law in Madrid, a draft code of air law, introduced by Fauchille, was discussed. This code restated the principle of the freedom of the air, subject to 'the right of subjacent states to take certain measures, to be determined, to insure their own security and that of the persons and property and their inhabitants.' Though adopted by a majority, the code met with opposition from a substantial number of members (Richards, 1912: 20; Colegrove, 1930: 43). Also in 1911, the Comité juridique international de l'aviation, founded by French jurists in 1909, held its first congress in Paris. The committee was essentially an international network of jurists favoring a global regime based on air freedom. Its first congress adopted a resolution warning that universal agreement would be impeded if the doctrine of state sovereignty over the air were admitted (Colegrove, 1930: 45). However, the opponents of air freedom among the legal profession also joined forces. The International Law Association, 'a legal society in which the British and American attitude predominated,' in 1913 adopted a resolution asserting the absolute sovereignty of subjacent states (Colegrove, 1930: 43–4).

With the advent of World War I, these early debates of international principles and regimes came to an abrupt end.

Unilateral action to safeguard national security prevailed over international collaboration.   *Everyone for themselves!*

Lawyers might not agree and diplomats might dodge a direct answer, but military and security questions had become immediately more important than any theoretical question of the advantage of free flight. Led by France, whose jurists had been the outstanding opponents of national airspace sovereignty, country after country of Europe declared its air boundaries closed. (Cooper, 1947: 22.)

## Drafting the convention of 1919

World War I drastically changed the context of bargaining. Not only did it tip the balance between legal and military considerations, but it also entailed the establishment of new transnational networks which were ultimately far more influential than the early networks of jurists.

As the peace conference assembled in Paris in the winter of 1918–19, the question of a postwar international aviation regime was placed on the agenda. The air forces of the allied powers had, since September 1917, been coordinated in an organization known as the Interallied Aviation Committee, as part of the Supreme War Council. At Paris, the secretary of this organization, Captain Boulanger, suggested that the Committee be reorganized and enlarged into a formal subcommittee of the peace conference charged with studying all aviation questions placed before the conference, including the international regulation of civil aviation. This proposal won general acceptance, and on 12 March 1919 a resolution was adopted to that effect, creating what came to be known as the Aeronautical Commission. To the five principal members of the commission — the British Empire, the United States, France, Italy and Japan — were added representatives of seven 'powers with limited interests': Belgium, Brazil, Cuba, Greece, Portugal, Rumania and Serbia. With the exception of three delegates from Italy, Japan and Cuba, all the members of the commission were military officers (Colegrove, 1930: 54–5; Cooper, 1947: 27).

The jurists had not left the scene entirely. Although most

of the experts assisting the Aeronautical Commission were military officers, its Legal Subcommittee was composed of civilian jurists, including some who had participated in the 1910 conference (Cooper, 1947: 28).

The major powers came unequally prepared for the regime discussions at the 1919 conference. Whereas Britain and France submitted detailed draft conventions, the United States had made no preparations in the field of civil aviation prior to the peace conference (Cooper, 1968: 141–2). The British, in particular, had planned for peace in the midst of war. In May 1917 a 'Civil Aerial Transport Committee' was appointed to prepare a report on 'the steps which should be taken with a view to the development and regulation after the War of aviation for civil and commercial purposes from a domestic, and imperial, and an international standpoint' (Cooper, 1947: 22).

The committee's report, which was placed before the British Parliament in 1918, contained a thorough discussion of conflicting theories. It was quite explicit about the advantages of air freedom from a commercial viewpoint and for improving communication between the scattered countries of the British Empire (Cooper, 1947: 23). Yet the final conclusion of the report was unequivocally in favor of airspace sovereignty:

The argument, however, for the doctrine of State sovereignty in the air space *usque ad coelum* is in the main a military one. Military considerations dictated the opposition of the British delegates to the proposals pressed by the German representatives at the Conference in Paris in 1910, and we understand that the views of the Foreign Office and of the naval and military advisers of the Crown are unchanged. To give to foreign aircraft, as a matter of acknowledged international law, the right to fly at will over the territory of the State would be to give them undesirable opportunities for espionage, and generally to limit 'the elementary right of a State to take each and every measure it considers necessary for self-preservation.' In time of war, moreover, the doctrine of the 'freedom of the air' above a certain altitude would give rise to most embarrassing questions for neutral States. They would actually be exposed to the risk of having aerial battles fought over their territory without being able to claim that their neutrality had been infringed. The case of the upper air presents no true analogy to the case of the high seas outside the limits of territorial waters. (Quoted in Cooper, 1947: 24.)

Although the report represented a broad consensus among different British ministries as well as between Britain and other parts of the Empire, one committee member submitted a minority view:

The British Isles are badly placed for aerial communication. Other nations bar the access to the great land masses associated to form the British Empire. A clear right of way free from restriction across France and Italy and Spain is essential to effective progress in inter-colonial air communications. Our self-interest, therefore, as a great Power lies towards an international settlement of air sovereignty. And for similar considerations our interest as a commercial and industrial people must lie in the same direction. The right to pass across other national territory without let or hindrance, relief from varying terms and conditions attaching to flight which may be onerous and irksome, the absence of Customs restraints or tariff restrictions, and generally the absence of the apparatus for hampering or artificially routing trade are all wanted. On all these grounds it is submitted that the case for an international settlement is strengthened. (Quoted in Cooper, 1947: 25–6.)

The French, too, had learned the bitter lessons of war and 'were in no mood to press Fauchille's doctrine of the freedom of the air' (Colegrove, 1930: 55). At the peace conference France was not represented by any of the great jurists, like Fauchille and Renault, who only a few years earlier had played the leading role in efforts to create an international regime based on air freedom (Colegrove, 1930: 57–8).

When the Aeronautical Commission met to consider an international aviation convention it had at its disposal three helpful documents: the aborted convention prepared at Paris in 1910 and new draft conventions prepared by the British and the French (Cooper, 1947: 28). In a curious reversal of roles, the British draft was, if anything, more liberal than the French. While insisting on airspace sovereignty, Britain proposed extremely broad privileges of flight, more or less corresponding to what later became known as the 'five freedoms' (Cooper, 1968: 143).

In six months the Aeronautical Commission managed to

prepare a complete convention, consisting of forty-three articles and eight annexes. On 27 September the completed convention was submitted to the Supreme Council of the peace conference, and on 13 October it was adopted and opened to signature (Colegrove, 1930: 57).

The loadstar of the negotiations was the principle of state sovereignty. The British proposal for wider freedoms was rejected. Thus the first article of the Paris Convention states unequivocally: 'The High Contracting Parties recognise that every Power has complete and exclusive sovereignty over the air space above its territory.' To be sure, the second article of the convention, in a seeming concession to the British viewpoint, obligates each signatory 'in time of peace to accord freedom of innocent passage above its territory to the aircraft of other contracting States' (Mance, 1943: 1–2; Cooper, 1947: 291–2). However, these rights were made meaningless by other parts of the convention, especially article 15 which provided that the establishment of 'international airways' be subject to the consent of the states flown over. No reason for refusal had to be given, nor was there any requirement that the right of overflight be given without distinction of nationality (Mance, 1943: 2). To quote Cooper (1947: 33), 'the victory for national control of the airspace was complete.'

## Conclusions

Whereas the perceptions of those who discussed a future aviation regime before World War I were colored by analogies with the law of the sea, immediate lessons of the war dominated the perceptions of the negotiators in 1919. The need to extend national sovereignty to the airspace was a common concern. To the negotiators, the situation obviously did not present itself as a choice between air freedom and sovereignty.

No issue linkage was attempted during the negotiations leading to the 1919 convention. The convention was negotiated separately from the peace treaty, and from the outset of the negotiations the issue of disarming Germany in the air was disconnected from the general questions of civil aviation after the war. It was generally felt that any attempt to incorporate an air convention in the peace treaty would indefinitely postpone the signing of the treaty (Colegrove, 1930: 54–5).

Although the outcome of the negotiations in 1919 cannot be characterized as a compromise, a process analysis shows that there were greater potentials for a compromise than structural and situational explanations would indicate. Some of the ideas of 1910 had, in fact, survived World War I; and there were significant differences of opinion within some of the negotiating states. The British and American delegates at Paris indicated a desire for the maximum freedom of commercial flight consistent with the retention of sovereignty over their airspace (Cooper, 1947: 136–8). But no effort was made in 1919 to form transnational coalitions among the proponents of air freedom. The negotiators in Paris, on the other hand, were members of an informal network created as a result of inter-allied cooperation in World War I. The earlier transnational network of jurists had to cede center stage to the military in the wake of a world war. The Paris Convention has been labelled 'the most remarkable treaty ever drawn up by a conference composed chiefly of military officers' (Colegrove, 1930: 57). One of the negotiators at Paris attributed the ability of the Aeronautical Commission to reach agreement to the fact that 'most of the members had learned, because of their experience as members of the Interallied Aviation Committee, how to work rapidly and harmoniously together,' concluding that 'it was no doubt thanks to this push, this ardor, this comradeship of the delegates, that the commission was able to lay down principles in a day, to set up the framework of the convention in a few weeks and to draw it up in less than four months' (Colegrove, 1930: 58).

# 6 Negotiating a new regime in the wake of World War II

Efforts to create a new international aviation regime began before World War II was over, and the negotiations were not conducted within the framework of a general peace conference, as in 1919. The number of aviation nations had increased significantly. In addition, a number of specialized aviation organizations had emerged.

## Organizational development during the interwar period

Already at the 1910 Paris conference, the French delegation had proposed the creation of an international organization, a 'Bureau international de Navigation aérienne,' as part of an aviation regime (Conférence internationale, 1910: 51–8). But since it was not formally included in the conference agenda, the French proposal was not subjected to any thorough discussion.

The Paris Convention of 1919, however, created a specialized IGO, the International Commission for Air Navigation (ICAN). Each nation that had ratified the convention was represented in this organization which was placed under the direction of the League of Nations. In practice, the League never attempted to exercise authority over ICAN which, for its part, never attempted to break away from the League (Mance, 1943: 19). ICAN was a European rather than a genuinely international organization, as the United States along with most of the other American republics and China did not adhere to the Paris Convention under which ICAN acted (Cooper, 1947: 158). The Havana Convention of 1928, to which the United States and nine other American republics adhered, differed from the Paris Convention in providing no permanent administrative machinery (UN, 1945: 2).

ICAN dealt primarily with technical questions related to the 1919 convention (cf. Colegrove, 1930: 72–3). It did much to standardize European flying (Cooper, 1947: 158) and served important informational functions. Kenneth Colegrove's (1930: 71) description of the kind of valuable practical information airmen could gather from ICAN's weekly *Bulletin of Information* is noteworthy, if nothing else, for the insight it provides into flying conditions of that time. Through the *Bulletin* one might learn, for instance:

that the Italian Ministry of Aeronautics has revised its prohibited areas and obligatory routes in crossing the Alps and flyers must take notice; that sheep are grazing on the landing field at Le Bourget and planes should be careful to avoid them; that the Cherbourg-Querqueville Aerodrome will be occupied by military formations on certain dates and private planes are barred; that plowing and leveling operations are in progress on the Croydon Aerodrome and pilots should avoid taxying beyond the boundary lights; that the Pisa Aerodrome is water-logged by heavy rains and is unfit for use; that the Rotterdam air-light is temporarily out of action; that the Italian Government has ordered a red flag to be displayed at the Furbara Aerodrome on the Rome-Civita Vecchia line whenever landing will be dangerous because of artillery fire; that Canada has organized a meteorological service and reports are obtainable at its offices in Toronto, Walkerville and St. Hubert; that a new system of air lights for night-flying has been installed along the Berlin-Hanover route; and that Denmark has issued a revised list of customs airdromes.

In 1919 yet another international organization came into being when a meeting of six European airlines founded the International Air Traffic Association (IATA). The organization was formed as a free and rather loose union of airlines, and the concept of a commercial cartel dividing the territory and sharing profits was rejected (Colegrove, 1930: 119–20; Brancker, 1977: 6). For several years IATA's geographical coverage was limited to Northern Europe, and there were rival organizations. French companies formed a free union embracing airlines in southern Europe, and a cartel, the Trans-Europa Union, operated in Central Europe. However, the French companies eventually became members of IATA and the cartel dissolved in 1925, whereupon the component corporations joined IATA (Colegrove, 1930: 120; Sampson, 1985: 47). By 1929 the organization had twenty-three members — virtually all the airlines of Europe. In 1938 the members of IATA agreed to elect their first North American member — Pan American Airways — and to hold their next meeting in New York. The plan had to be abandoned as a result of the outbreak of World War II. IATA, which by 1939 numbered thirty-three members, including carriers from North and South America, Asia and Africa, did not develop into a global organization.

IATA's main concern was the commercial organization of European air services. The organization managed to reach certain agreements on the procedures and forms to be used for handling traffic and also pursued standardization in technical matters (Mance, 1943: 22; Brancker, 1977: 7).

In addition to ICAN and IATA, a number of private associations dealt with aviation matters during the interwar period. The various associations of international lawyers survived World War I. The Institute of International Law continued to promote air freedom, while admitting the sovereignty of subjacent states; the International Law Association approved the 1919 convention, while urging amendments in order to eliminate the clauses inspired by the war and to pave the way for the adherence of more states; and the Comité juridique international de l'aviation resumed its task of constructing a code of air law (Colegrove, 1930: 114–17). CITEJA (Comité International Technique d'Experts Juridiques Aérien) was established in 1926 as an advisory body to ICAN on the coordination of domestic air laws. CITEJA included non-members of ICAN, such as the United States and the Soviet Union (Tombs, 1936: 125–7). Furthermore, the International Chamber of Commerce, founded in 1921, took a particular interest in problems of international communication. In 1923, it set up a Committee on Air Transport which issued recommendations to governments concerning such matters as the unification of air law and the promotion of air mail services (Colegrove, 1930: 117–19; Mance, 1943: 23–4).

A few regional aviation organizations were created, mainly in Europe. The International Aeronautical Conference (CAI), consisting of nine European countries, originated as a series of Anglo-French air conferences. In the 1930s the Mediterranean Air Conference and the Baltic and Balkan States Air Conference were created, with partly overlapping memberships (Tombs, 1936: 143–5). CAI tended to become the originating body in the more technical aspects of aviation. Frequently, proposals originating in CAI were subsequently adopted at ICAN meetings, where the necessary alterations would be made to render them applicable worldwide (Mance, 1943: 21).

In brief, the creation of international organizations on the heels of World War I was of limited *political* significance. To be sure, in air transport as in other fields, the interwar experiments in international organization represented embryos of the structures which were to emerge from World War II. But they were restricted in several important respects.

First, ICAN and IATA as well as other organizations concentrated their efforts in the field of standardization.

It is easy to forget these days that at that time air transport was virtually the only form of transport which required standardisation on a general international basis, so that it was breaking very new ground in attempting it. The railways had, of course, accepted standard gauge and freight wagons and coaches moved internationally, but locomotives tended to stay in their own countries. It may sound very elementary now, but it was then necessary to make a recommendation to the effect that throttle controls on all aircraft should be so arranged that a push forward meant acceleration and push back meant slowing down. The same kind of apparently elementary recommendations were needed in almost all technical matters, including such things as fuel intakes, other aircraft instrumentation and controls, etc. (Brancker, 1977: 7.)

Second, the interwar organizations had limited geographical scope. Much work was done to standardize European air transport, but several important aviation nations, including the United States, remained outside ICAN. Similarly, it was only shortly before World War II that non-European airlines began to join IATA.

Third, these early organizations by and large lacked effective secretariats and had to rely on the individual members for action (cf. Tombs, 1936: 143–4; Mance, 1943: 21; Brancker, 1977: 8). This fact, in combination with the essentially nonpolitical role and limited geographical scope of the organizations, explains why no significant transnational networks were built around them. Thus, when discussions about the future international aviation regime began toward the end of World War II, there was no informal network to mediate state interests.

## Negotiating the Chicago-Bermuda regime

'By 1943 men began to think of postwar aviation' (Cooper, 1947: 158). The main allies in the war, the United States and Britain, took center stage in the early planning for peacetime air transport, with other members of the British Commonwealth assuming important roles. World War II was a time of civil-military partnership in aviation. In the US Air Transport Command (ATC), established in 1942, key airline executives occupied important posts (Thayer, 1965: 50). The ATC, in organizing a strategic airlift system, 'carried the American air flag to every corner of the globe, conducting scheduled transport operations on a scale unmatched or even approached by any other nation in the world' (Cook, 1945: 15). This, of course, represented an important asset for the Americans when negotiating the postwar aviation regime. In the words of the US Under Secretary of War Robert Patterson, the ATC service 'should operate with economy, but it should be so organized as to demonstrate the efficiency of this country in the air transportation field and should compare favorably with the air transport services operated by any of the other nations' (Thayer, 1965: 56).

The British obviously viewed it differently. In December 1942, Captain Balfour said in the House of Commons (Smith, 1950: 133): 'To use a colloquialism, we have agreed on the highest level with the Americans that as regards routes they are running which may have commercial values, "all bets are off" at the end of the war.'

President Roosevelt began to discuss aviation policy with Prime Minister Churchill at Quebec in September 1943 (Smith, 1950: 150; Berle, 1973: 483). Informal talks between representatives of the countries of the British Commonwealth took place in October 1943 (UN, 1945: 3), and members of the

Commonwealth subsequently took some important initiatives. On 21 January 1944, Australia and New Zealand signed
a 'Cooperation Agreement,' in which the two countries
expressed their view that a new universal convention should
be adopted and that 'the air services using the international
trunk routes should be operated by an international air
transport authority' (Cooper, 1947: 159–60). Two months
later, Canada presented a draft convention, proposing an
international authority to fix routes, frequencies and rates,
and to issue permits for international operators. In addition,
the draft prescribed a multilateral exchange of transit and
certain trading privileges (Cooper, 1947: 160–1).

Through diplomatic correspondence it became clear that
the Americans and the British had different ideas as to how
a new aviation regime might be developed.

The British proposed a bilateral or face-to-face negotiation for
allocation of world routes, but the Americans insisted on including
the Canadians in the discussion because of the significance of the
Canadian corridor on the Atlantic routes. It was also suggested that
the President favored inviting Russia, China, and Brazil to such a
meeting because of their strategic positions on the world air map.
The British agreed, but insisted quite logically that all members of
the empire had as much right to participate as countries like China
and Brazil. (Smith, 1950: 153.)

The 'Big Two' eventually agreed to hold a series of
exploratory meetings, first with each other, and then with
other nations concerned in air commerce. In April, 1944,
Adolf Berle, US Assistant Secretary of State, visited Ottawa
and London. Throughout the summer US representatives
held informal bilateral consultations with other aviation
countries, including the Soviet Union, China, the
Netherlands and leading Latin American countries. Similar
talks were initiated by the British government (UN, 1945: 3;
Smith, 1950: 154–5).

The successful allied offensive through Normandy added
urgency to the issue. 'It looked as though the preparatory
work done might have come too late, and that scheduled civil
flying might have to begin *ad hoc* without waiting for the new
rules' (UN, 1945: 3). In June 1944, the US Civil Aeronautics
Board announced the international routes for which Am-

erican carriers made claims. The British insisted on holding a multilateral conference, and the Canadian government made a similar request. The Americans had little interest in such a meeting at that time, but the British made it clear that, if the Americans did not call a conference immediately, they would issue their own invitations. A diplomatic note of 29 August outlined the British position: 'If, for domestic reasons, you should find it difficult to hold a conference in Washington at the present time, we shall understand your position and stand ready to call a conference ourselves in London' (Smith, 1950: 158).

Spurred on by the British, the US government then invited all the nations of the world except enemy or enemy-held countries to meet in Chicago on 1 November 1944. One week before the Chicago conference convened, the Commonwealth countries held joint air policy talks in Montreal. These failed to achieve any unanimity of views on the issues to be discussed at Chicago (Cook, 1945: 31).

With no Commonwealth united front, the delegates at Chicago had before them four different proposals, submitted by New Zealand and Australia, Canada, Britain and the United States, respectively. The delegations from Australia and New Zealand presented and argued their case for 'the establishment of an international air transport authority which would be responsible for the operation of air services on prescribed international trunk routes and which would own the aircraft and ancillary equipment employed on these routes' (US Department of State, 1948: 550).

Another, less far-reaching plan for international coopera-tion in the air was submitted by Canada. In the Canadian view, merely assigning exclusive power to an international body answered no questions. Canada's chief negotiator told the delegates at Chicago that 'an international air authority established along the lines of the Civil Aeronautics Board of the United States is the principal proposal which Canada places before this conference' (US Department of State, 1948: 67).

At the same time, the Canadians initiated the discussion of different 'freedoms of the air' by suggesting that by multilateral convention each nation should grant other na-tions (1) the right to fly across its territory without landing;

(2) the right to land for servicing; (3) the right to carry passengers, mail and cargo from the country of origin to any place in the world; and (4) the right to bring passengers, mail and cargo back to the country of origin from any place in the world (US Department of State, 1948: 67).

The Canadians declared themselves 'firm believers in healthy competition' yet 'convinced that it will develop most fruitfully under an international authority' (US Department of State, 1948: 67):

We think that it is unrealistic to talk in terms of a multilateral grant of freedom of air transport and commercial outlet, unless those grants of air freedom are accompanied by the establishment of an effective international authority, with power, in the ultimate resort, to regulate frequencies and to fix rates. Without an effective international regulatory authority, mere freedoms of the air would lead either to unbridled competition, or to the domination of the airways of the world by a few. (US Department of State, 1948: 73.)

The British position was laid down in a White Paper on 'International Air Transport' presented in Parliament just  prior to the Chicago conference and later placed before the conference. The British proposal, like the Canadian, envisaged an international body which should do for the world what the CAB had done for the United States. In fact, the British plan went even further than the Canadian one, by empowering the international authority to regulate the number of flights each company might make, determine the percentage of traffic which each country's airlines might carry in any region, and allocate certain routes to certain countries to the exclusion of others (Berle, 1945: 6). Whereas Canada proposed international cooperation on the basis of freedom of opportunity, Britain's plan was based on rigid allocation and regulation.

To the British, regulation seemed more important than internationalization. For one thing, the British proposal offered no provisions for the composition or decision-making rules of the international regulatory body (Thornton, 1970: 26–7). Also, the arguments of the British delegates emphasized the regulatory aspects of their proposal. Strict regulation was needed, first, to 'ensure equitable participation by the various countries engaged in international air transport' (UK Secretary of State for Air, 1944: 3; US Department of State, 1948: 568). Behind this argument was the understandable fear that the United States would monopolize the world air transport of the immediate future. The British negotiators pointed out that international operations were vital to European airlines, most European air traffic being international rather than domestic. In the United States, by contrast, domestic airlines carried eight or nine times as much traffic as the international routes (Smith, 1950: 169).

Another British argument stressed the necessity to 'maintain broad equilibrium between the world's air transport capacity and the traffic offering' (UK Secretary of State for Air, 1944: 3; US Department of State, 1948: 568). The British feared that without strict control international services would be put into operation greatly exceeding the actual traffic demands. This, in turn, would inevitably lead to subsidy races and rate wars (cf. Morgan, 1945: 10).

Moreover, security considerations loomed large in Britain's argument. The future international regime should, according to the British White Paper, 'contribute to world security' (UK Secretary of State for Air, 1944: 3; US Department of State, 1948: 568). The British chief negotiator at Chicago, Lord Swinton, expressed it thus (US Department of State, 1948: 63):

In these years of war, looking at the vast destruction which air forces have wrought and the ever increasing range and potentiality of aircraft, it is natural that many should be more impressed by the menace of the air than by its power for good. They feel, and indeed they feel rightly, that the whole future of security is bound up with the air.

The United States, finally, envisaged an international organization with limited technical and safety functions, leaving each nation with wide and unregulated competitive powers. On the subject of internationalization, the chief US negotiator, Adolf Berle, stated (US Department of State, 1948: 545):

Everyone of us in this room knows that we should be glad if we could give effect to the kind of plan that Australia and New Zealand have thus bravely and appropriately offered but everyone of us knows that it will require years of work before we can bring about such a situation. Hoping for the ideal, as we do, recognizing the real situation as we must, are we not obliged to tread the slower and more painful path of working together in the simplest steps making for world peace before we undertake the faster and more complicated task of putting the interest of many peoples in the hands of an instrument still unfashioned and whose potentialities are still unknown?

The American position was predicated upon the belief that the fewer restrictions placed on international air commerce, the faster it would grow, to the benefit of all. International aviation should be guided by free competition rather than international regulation. The counter-arguments to the view that the US position was merely an attempt to capitalize on its lead in air transport, have been summarized by one of the members of the American delegation (Burden, 1945: 18):

We recognize that some will say that we are motivated by self-interest in proposing a policy which would permit the most efficient operator to attract the most traffic. True, we have a technical headstart over the war-ravaged countries of Europe because of our huge production of transport airplanes and our wide experience in long-distance operation. We have no desire to take unfair advantage of this position and have announced our willingness to make our transport aircraft available, as soon as they can be spared from war work, to all countries which recognize the right of friendly intercourse with others. We point out that our supremacy in air transport is not solely due to the accidents of war; we were leaders in the field long before 1939. We feel that it would be criminal to condemn world air transport to permanent restriction in an attempt to offset a temporary advantage held by one country.

These were the four main proposals, as the Chicago conference began. The Soviet decision, at the last minute, not to attend the conference came as a surprise, and the Soviet position remained unknown. To this day, we can only speculate about the reasons behind the Soviet move. It has been suggested that the Soviet Union at that time had little interest in international aviation, that its first priority was domestic reconstruction (Thornton, 1970: 22). Furthermore, the various proposals presented prior to the conference suggested outcomes which would run counter to Soviet interests. Adoption of the American approach would entail the right of other countries to fly freely into Soviet airspace; an agreement along the lines of the Commonwealth proposals would mean that the liberty of action of the Russian authorities would be restrained by the decisions of an international organization. Either alternative must have appeared unacceptable from the Soviet point of view (cf. Johnson, 1972: 237–8).

The initial positions of the participants in the Chicago conference can be placed along the two dimensions suggested in the discussion of situational explanations in the previous chapter: international/national authority and regulation/competition. If we regard these as continua rather than either/or dichotomies, the proposals of Australia-New Zealand, Canada, Britain and the United States can be grouped as in Figure 8.

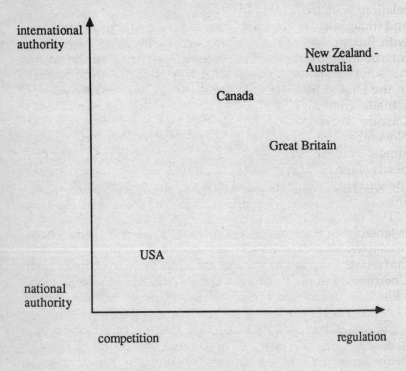

**Figure 8.** National proposals at Chicago

Discussions at Chicago came to center around the American and British proposals which were opposites on both dimensions. The Australian-New Zealand draft convention was discarded as too radical. In opposing it, the Brazilian delegate said that 'our times are not yet ripe for the internationalization of aviation and perhaps the time will never be ripe for it' (US Department of State, 1948: 544). A Brazilian motion not to negotiate on the basis of the Australia-New Zealand plan was supported by the United States.

As Figure 8 suggests, Canada was in a potential mediator position. The Canadians found common ground with American thought in their support of competition, yet shared the British view of the need for a strong international authority. Like Britain, Canada wanted international air routes to be 'divided fairly and equitably between the various member states' (US Department of State, 1948: 68). Canada had close relations with the United States geographically, commercially and financially, at the same time as it had strong cultural ties with Britain. Moreover, Canada had a stake in the future of international aviation because 'the main airway of the world cut across Canada, and many of the strategic traffic centers in the United States would some day be reached by way of Canada' (Smith, 1950: 169–70). It was therefore natural that Canada strived to find a compromise solution. On 12 November the Canadian delegation began 'eleven days of almost continuous day and night conversations' with the heads of the US and British delegations which, though closing the gap between the two, fell short of success (Cook, 1945: 18).

The clash between the United States and Britain was ostensibly one of divergent principles. But behind these principles were conflicts of interest between the 'haves' and 'have-nots,' as perceptively expressed by Welch Pogue, Chairman of the US CAB after the war (quoted in Smith, 1950: 140):

It would be the height of naiveté to contend that the United States desires an 'open sky' primarily to improve the welfare of mankind. By the same token, it would be unfair to contend that the refusal of Great Britain or any other nation to conform to our views is necessarily reprehensible. Once again we are confronted with an *what's good for the US is necessarily good for all.*

attempt to rationalize an international problem on the notably fallacious and dangerous theory that since the 'open sky' principle would conform to the requirements of the United States, it would be acceptable to the rest of the world — regardless of any political or economic incompatibilities that may exist. This line of reasoning is usually accompanied by carefully chosen slogans concerning human progress and liberty, which have the effect of putting the nations that would oppose it in the position of being antisocial.

A Canadian study (quoted in Van Zandt, 1944: 56) describes the motives behind the British position with similar candor. 'The United Kingdom and other countries will be anxious to obtain the right of access to the rich traffic of the United States,' but because of a lower traffic potential 'might find difficulties in competition with the United States in a world of unregulated freedom of transit and bilateral bargaining over traffic.' Hence, by favoring restrictions on both freedom of transit and trade, 'the United Kingdom and other countries might hope . . . to be assured of a greater share of international air transport.'

This conflict of interest was aggravated by a clash of personalities between the heads of the American and British delegations, Adolf Berle and Lord Swinton. Berle has been described as 'aggressive, brilliant in his grasp of intricate problems, and leftish in his thinking on aviation' (Smith, 1950: 164); he is said to have had an engrained 'suspicion of British imperialism and the European fondness for cartels' (Sampson, 1985: 81). Lord Swinton, a long-standing ally of Churchill, who had just returned from being resident minister in West Africa, has been labelled 'the antithesis of the American leader,' 'known to have little regard for Americans,' and 'even further to the right on aviation matters than Berle was to the left' (Smith, 1950: 165, 166). According to Anthony Sampson (1985: 83):

After Swinton met Berle in Chicago he told his wife that Berle was 'easily the most disagreeable person with whom I have ever negotiated,' while Berle thought Swinton was 'arrogant and inflexible, not having quite appreciated the difference between the atmosphere in the Gulf of Guinea and that of the shores of Lake Michigan.' (cf. Berle, 1973: 503.)

This made for unbridled, acrimonious exchanges. One member of the US delegation has put it thus:

A British proposal presented as a means of avoiding cutthroat competition and achieving decent order in the air has been unflatteringly called 'cartelism.' Conversely, proposals which their American advocates think offer the best air transportation for the whole world, and the greatest assurance that services will develop in accordance with the needs of the customers, are labelled in some transatlantic comment as 'economic imperialism.' (Warner, 1945: 32.)

Rather than mutual persuasion attempts, 'one of the main activities at Chicago was lining up recruits for the respective camps' (Smith, 1950: 171). The British Commonwealth nations in general stuck together and were supported by France, Belgium and some other European countries. The United States was backed by the Latin American nations, China, Norway, Sweden and the Netherlands, among others (Cook, 1945: 18).

The substantive discussions concentrated on two broad agenda items: the idea of 'freedoms of the air,' on the one hand, and frequency and capacity, on the other.

At the outset of the negotiations, the United States aimed at a general exchange of transit privileges as a means of facilitating subsequent bilateral negotiations for international air routes. But when Canada put forward the idea of 'four freedoms,' the possibility arose of lifting aviation out of bilateralism altogether (Cook, 1945: 13). The United States then countered with a proposal to include a 'fifth freedom' — the freedom for a foreign plane to carry traffic between countries outside its own.

The US view was that through lines could not develop profitably on terminal traffic alone, as provided under the Canadian formula. This applied, in particular, to US airlines. A regime based on the four freedoms only might have stopped American operations at the western gateways of Europe and the northern points of Latin America.

An airline operating a long route under this Canadian formula would fly with a constantly growing number of empty seats. For example, a plane from New York to Cairo via London, Paris,

Geneva, and Rome would drop off at each city the passengers booked to that point and take on none, thus probably arriving at Cairo with perhaps two or three seats occupied. Between New York and Buenos Aires, for instance, only 15 percent of the traffic is through traffic, and therefore we should be able to operate only about one plane a week on that trade route. Such a restriction would strangle the lines of every country except those operated for political reasons with heavy government subsidies. (Morgan, 1945: 12–13.)

The British were not willing to grant fifth-freedom privileges, arguing that the long-haul (read: American) airlines would carry most of the traffic and prevent other national airlines from building a satisfactory route network. The American counter-argument was that 'a limitation on carrying intermediate traffic hardly seems consistent with the theory that one of the main purposes of international regulation is to prevent the running of largely empty aircraft' (Burden, 1945: 20).

The question of freedoms of the air became linked to the issue of frequencies and capacity. In the US view, airlines ought to be free to determine how often and with what kind of aircraft they would operate every route. The British and the Canadians, however, predicated their willingness to grant four freedoms on close controls over frequencies and capacity. Britain proposed that traffic quotas be set for each operator, based on past records. Canada suggested an 'escalation' formula, according to which an airline would be allowed to increase its capacity or frequency only when the existing services had a load factor (the ratio of filled seats to empty seats) of 65 percent (Cook, 1945: 14).

Although the quota system did not tally with the American concept of free competition, the Americans showed some willingness to make concessions. They were prepared to accept a slightly more liberal version of the Canadian escalation proposal, in which airlines with traffic exceeding a 60 percent load factor would be entitled to additional flights. The American provision that fifth-freedom traffic be included when computing load factors was resisted by Britain. Only the traffic carried direct from the airline's home country, not intermediate traffic picked up *en route*, should count in establishing load factors, according to the British (Cook, 1945: 18–19; Burden, 1945: 20).

Another point at issue was whether escalation would be automatic under a fixed formula or be determined by an international air authority, as Britain insisted over American opposition.

Thus, although some rapprochement was achieved in the secret tripartite talks, no compromise was reached. Stokeley Morgan, the Secretary-General of the American delegation, reminisces (quoted in Smith, 1950: 170–1):

It is true that during the closed sessions of the British, American, and Canadian delegates, during which the rest of the conference impatiently marked time and grew hotter and hotter under the collar, we had discussions and reached tentative agreement on a great many of the points at issue, but we always stressed the fact that this was all tentative, subject to reconsideration (as it would have been), and we were simply passing questions on to others, not considering them in any way as closed issues. From start to finish it was understood that everything depended upon a final agreement on Fifth Freedom traffic and minimum regulation.

Nor did an exchange of personal letters between Roosevelt and Churchill bring any concrete results. Roosevelt referred to Britain's request for capacity limitations as 'a form of strangulation' which would 'place a dead hand on the use of the great air trade-routes.' Churchill, for his part, reminded Roosevelt of America's virtual monopoly of transport aircraft and appealed to wartime unity. 'Can we not reach agreement,' asked Churchill, 'when great battles in which our troops are fighting side by side are at their height?' (Sampson, 1985: 85–7).

After three weeks, the Chicago conference seemed to have reached an impasse. Pressures for adjournment built up among the American and British delegates. By 22 November the conference seemed on the verge of failure, and only impassioned and well-orchestrated pleas by New York Mayor La Guardia and Herbert Symington, head of Trans-Canada Air Lines, convinced the delegates to keep negotiating (Smith, 1950: 175–6; cf. US Department of State, 1948: 453, 464–6). Yet in the absence of any progress, the US and British delegations were ready to give up the negotiations as hopeless on 1 December. Again, Mayor La Guardia took the floor, this time with a suggestion for a workable compromise.

'We've built the hangar,' he began, 'we have all the navigation instruments; we've provided for weather reports; but we haven't got a plane' (US Department of State, 1948: 493). Just because the United States and Great Britain could not agree on the controversial fifth-freedom rights was no reason to jettison the four other freedoms, he argued: 'Give us half a loaf, give the people of the world some hope, put Freedoms 1 and 2 in the Convention or Interim Agreement' (US Department of State, 1948: 497). The mayor's proposal got an immediate response. The Dutch delegation moved that the first two freedoms — the rights of transit and service stops — should be written as a separate document. After some initial confusion, this proposal met with general support and was adopted the following day (US Department of State, 1948: 514; Smith, 1950: 182–3; Berle, 1973: 507–8).

In the recollection of Stokeley Morgan of the US delegation (quoted in Smith, 1950: 183–4):

it was Lord Swinton who, perhaps resignedly and perhaps inadvertently, made the statement in one of the committee meetings that while Britain still must insist on her general policy with regard to commercial traffic, she should have no objection to granting the first two freedoms without any strings attached.

This was seized upon by the Dutch delegate, much to the dismay of the Canadians: 'Symington was practically livid because of course Canada's main bargaining position was the withholding of transit privileges' (Smith, 1950: 184). In fact, a Canadian study prepared prior to the Chicago conference had warned that Canada, by granting multilateral rights of transit, would give what the United States needed most and have little left to bargain with; Canada 'would be giving up its strongest bargaining point, since Canada will not have a great deal of traffic to offer, although, because of geographical position, many international airlines will wish to cross her territory' (Van Zandt, 1944: 61).

In the end, however, Canada went along. When the Chicago conference was adjourned on 7 December 1944, it had produced four different documents for signature: (1) a Convention on International Civil Aviation which, among other things, reaffirmed the basic principle of the 'complete and exclusive sovereignty' over national airspace; (2) an Interim Agreement on International Civil Aviation, providing for the establishment of PICAO (the Provisional International Civil Aviation Organization) whose principal function was to prepare aviation standards for the consideration of the coming permanent organization ICAO; (3) an International Air Services Transit Agreement, also called the Two Freedoms Agreement; and (4) an International Air Transport Agreement, also called the Five Freedoms Agreement.

The Chicago conference could be considered a failure, insofar as it did not secure the five freedoms of the air or solve the crucial issues of rates and frequencies. On the other hand, it could be labelled a success, insofar as it opened up world routes and eased the restrictions imposed on international air transport in the years before Chicago (cf. Smith, 1950: 191). With a hyperbole befitting the occasion, conference chairman Adolf Berle expressed it thus in his concluding speech (US Department of State, 1948: 111):

We met in the seventeenth century in the air. We close in the twentieth century in the air. We met in an era of diplomatic intrigue and private and monopolistic privilege. We close in an era of open covenants and equal opportunity and status.

In brief, the developments and results of the Chicago conference were controversial. The positions of the chief state actors at Chicago did not necessarily represent national consensus. There were from the outset internal disagreements with potentials for cross-national coalitions — potentials which do not seem to have been exploited in the bargaining process.

For one thing, there were 'internationalists' on both sides of the Atlantic, whose sympathies lay with the Australia-New Zealand plan. In the United States they were represented by such idealists as Henry Wallace, Roosevelt's Vice-President, who envisaged 'a network of globe-girdling airways' to be operated by 'the air arm of the United Nations peace force' (quoted in Hutchison, 1944: 19), and Wendell Willkie, Roosevelt's rival for the presidency in 1940, who became a prominent spokesman for the 'one world' idea. 'The modern airplane creates a new geographical dimension,' Willkie said in 1943: 'A navigable ocean of air blankets the whole surface of the globe. There are no distant places any longer: the world is small and the world is one' (quoted in Sampson, 1985: 78).

An authoritative study by the British Brigadier-General Sir Osborne Mance (1943), written under the auspices of the Royal Institute of International Affairs, expressed sympathy for the idea of a powerful international organization owning and controlling airlines. Furthermore, the agreement between the Labor governments of Australia and New Zealand in early 1944 had immediate repercussions in Britain. In April 1944, the British Labour Party, then in opposition, published a pamphlet, *Wings for Peace*, calling for the internationalization of air transport:

In particular, we urge that the trunk air lines round the world — 'World Airways' — should be owned and operated as a public service by a body responsible to the World Air Authority and competent to act as trustee for all the peoples, whether they happen to be able to run an aircraft industry or not. Militant nationalism should have no part, as hitherto, in the opening up of the world's air routes. (Labour Party, 1944: 21.)

Similarly, there were those in Canada who argued for a more radical approach than that taken by their government. For instance, in June 1944 Air Force Marshal William Bishop published a book entitled *Winged Peace*, in which he called for 'world operation of world airways' (Bishop, 1944: 171).

However, other voices were ultimately more influential in shaping the negotiating positions of these countries. While the internationalist current was particularly strong in Britain, there were other, less idealistic pressures on the aviation policy-makers. A committee representing industrial and commercial interests was appointed in early 1943 to investigate the postwar prospects of British air transport. Its report emphasized the need for neutralizing the American dominance in the field, and recommended immediate bilateral negotiations with the United States.

The aim of these negotiations should be to establish the principle that the international air services of the United States and the British Empire should be based on parity in terms of a mutually acceptable yardstick. When this preliminary agreement has been reached, discussions should take place with Russia and China and then the remainder of the United Nations to decide what quantitative relation this parity should bear to the air transport services of other countries. (Van Zandt, 1944: 55.)

There were differences concerning tactics as well. Lord Beaverbrook was replaced as Minister for Aviation by Lord Swinton shortly before the Chicago conference. Beaverbrook had assumed that a united empire front would bring the Americans to terms, and that a soft attitude toward the United States would therefore be preferable. The lack of Commonwealth unity damaged his prestige, and Swinton had been one of his severest critics (Smith, 1950: 165).

As a result of this internal tug-of-war, the British came less than adequately prepared to Chicago (Smith, 1950: 164; Sampson, 1985: 82–3). Swinton was newly installed in his office: 'Had he been a genius as a statesman he still could not have grasped the issues in the short interval between his appointment as the new Minister of Civil Aviation and his appearance in Chicago. And Lord Swinton was not a genius' (Smith, 1950: 164). Furthermore, some of the leading British representatives at Chicago did not attend delegation meetings because of other, more pressing, business (Sampson, 1985: 83).

In the United States there was a continuous struggle between what Henry Ladd Smith (1950: 134–8) has labelled 'imperialists' and 'merchant airmen.' The imperialists believed that, by winning the war, America had a 'manifest destiny' to dominate the air. The much-publicized freshman speech of Connecticut Congresswoman Clare Booth Luce in February 1943 is representative of this school of thought (quoted in Smith, 1950: 129):

Our American pilots ... know that America, which produced the Wright brothers and Lindbergh and Rickenbacker, and scores upon scores of air pioneers and heroes, has not only the tools, but the technical genius and the industrial capacity — in short everything it takes — to let American pilots and passengers go anywhere in the world. For the postwar air policy of these hundreds of thousands of young airminded Americans is quite simple. It is: 'We want to fly everywhere. Period.'

The 'merchant airmen,' by contrast, were willing to concede the necessity of some international cooperation and thus to sacrifice a certain amount of independence in exchange for order in international aviation. This kind of thinking informed policy-making in the White House during the later stage of World War II. Adolf Berle, who was later to lead the American delegation at Chicago, played a crucial role in planning postwar aviation policy. Drafted by Roosevelt as one of the original braintrusters, he was close to the President and became Chairman of an Interdepartmental Committee on Aviation, appointed in 1941 (Smith, 1950: 146–7, 149). Another key figure was Lloyd Welch Pogue, Chairman of the Civil Aeronautics Board. Like Berle, he advocated the open-skies principle. Unlike Berle, he believed that open skies could best be achieved through bilateral negotiations rather than multilateral agreements (Smith, 1950: 148).

Both Berle and Pogue prepared reports for the President which denounced the restrictive policies of the imperialist school and recommended that the United States abandon some of its air sovereignty for the benefit of the world (Smith, 1950: 149–50). On the basis of these reports, President Roosevelt drafted his own proposals for postwar air commerce. He favored a free exchange of transit and landing rights. Also, he decided that American international air transport should not be handled by a single line, although 'certain companies — to speak frankly, Pan American — wanted all the business' (cf. Smith, 1950: 151–2).

The most formidable opponent to the president's plan was indeed Pan Am, personified by its autocratic chairman Juan Trippe, sometimes called the 'Emperor of the Air' (Sampson, 1985: 74). William Burden, Assistant Secretary of Commerce in charge of aviation matters and a member of the US delegation at Chicago, has described Pan Am's dissent in diplomatic terms:

A small segment of informed American opinion, led by Pan American Airways, disagrees with [the official US] position and maintains that — regardless of the effect on the world as a whole — the self-interest of the United States would be best served by continuing the prewar system of bilateral negotiation. Pan American argues that foreign shipping companies enjoy a tremendous competitive advantage over United States lines because of lower labor costs, and that the same situation will develop in air transport unless the entry of foreign airlines into the United States is severely restricted. (Burden, 1945: 18.)

The 'small segment of informed American opinion' included influential senators, such as Owen Brewster, jokingly called 'the Senator from Pan Am,' and Patrick McCarran, a friend of Trippe's (cf. Smith, 1950: 147; Sampson, 1985: 99, 102). Brewster, who was on the US delegation at Chicago, apparently reported the delegation's decisions to Pan Am and the American press (Berle, 1973: 500–1). Adolf Berle (1973: 502) lamented that 'it is hard enough fighting things out with the British, without having a member of your own Delegation, who announced that he is in the opposition, try to make political capital out of interior affairs.'

In addition to influencing domestic opinion leaders, Pan Am tried to strike a secret deal with the British Overseas Airways Corporation (BOAC) on the eve of the Chicago conference (Smith, 1950: 167, 178). In late June 1944, Berle (1973: 487–8) wrote in his diary:

We know that Trippe of Pan American Airways negotiated with [Alfred Cecil] Critchley of BOAC when Critchley was in the country some months ago. They agreed, roughly, that Pan American would have the cream of the North Atlantic traffic; and would stay out of the continent of Europe, BOAC staying out of South America except for a limited entry. Critchley had no authority to make this agreement and Beaverbrook suspected him and had him shadowed by the British Intelligence. The report of the deal reached Beaverbrook via the Intelligence . . . and it was later confirmed by Critchley, whereupon Beaverbrook directed that it all be called off. But, so far as the two groups are concerned, both appear to have endeavored to carry it out if they could.

The War Department was also critical of the official US approach to the Chicago negotiations. In a letter of 11 October 1944 (quoted in US Senate, 1945: 267–8), the Secretary of War complained to the Secretary of State that his department had not been allowed to participate in, or comment on, the preparation of the American position:

It is the opinion of this Department that international security and the national defense interests of this country require that in the postwar period the United States have the world's foremost air-transport system. In view of the present preeminent position of our military air-transport system, the experience of our civil air carriers, the number and technical qualifications of our operating personnel, and the state of development of our aircraft industry, the realization of this objective is inevitable unless these advantages are bartered away. The procedures envisaged by the invitation to the Conference and the agenda prepared by the State Department for presentation at the Conference ... are entirely inappropriate to retain for the United States its present ascendant position in the field.

The struggle and discord extended to the American delegation at the Chicago conference. Adolf Berle, who headed the delegation, was unpopular with many aviation leaders because of his identification with the New Deal; 'he was certainly on Pan American Airways' "go-to-hell" list' (Smith, 1950: 147). Senators Brewster and Josiah Bailey were not in favor of the course set by Berle and the President; they charged that Berle was eroding America's bargaining strength by insisting on multilateral agreements. CAB Chairman Pogue did not see eye-to-eye with Berle; he, too, preferred a bilateral approach and was sometimes kept in the dark about Berle's negotiating tactics (Smith, 1950: 164–5, 177, 192). In short, the US representatives did not act as a unit.

While negotiations were in progress at Chicago, Secretary of State Cordell Hull was forced to retire for health reasons. For an interim period the Department of State was led by Edward Stettinius, Juan Trippe's brother-in-law. Only five days before the conclusion of the Chicago conference, the White House announced that Adolf Berle had resigned as Assistant Secretary of State. To be sure, he remained as head of the US delegation at Chicago but, as noted by one observer (Smith, 1950: 179):

the change in his status might well have been taken by his adversaries as a sign that Berle's views did not necessarily reflect the official policy of the United States. If the resignation announcement had not been a slap, why could it not have been delayed the five days until the critical agreements were signed and the delegates were homeward bound?

The demonstrative dismissal of Berle heralded new disagreements after the conclusion of the Chicago conference. Even before the conference was over, one of the congressional representatives on the US delegation, Senator Brewster, registered his dissent in a letter to Berle; he would 'not assent to a plan that proposes to give to the world 51 franchises to fly into the United States — the richest potential market for air travel in the world, since it seems generally expected that Americans will furnish perhaps 75 percent of international air travel in the decade following the war' (quoted in US Senate, 1945: 343).

Brewster's letter heralded the criticism to come, as the results of the Chicago conference were considered by the US Congress. The Senate Foreign Relations Committee was suspicious of the manner in which the aviation documents had been negotiated at Chicago. The State Department intended to classify three of the four documents as 'executive agreements,' which did not require consent of the Senate. Only the Convention was an obvious treaty matter. There was widespread sentiment in the Senate that this was an abuse of executive agreements, that 'no agreements of this character should be made except in the form of treaties to be considered and ratified by the Senate' (US Senate, 1946: 12).

Hearings in the Foreign Relations Committee dragged on. The adversaries of the Chicago documents, notably Pan Am, were active lobbying on Capitol Hill. One senator testified in the hearings to being 'buttonholed and lobbied' by unnamed private aviation companies, adding:

I am just as much against an American cartel and an American monopoly as I am against any other cartel or any other monopoly, and I think this question ought to be settled on its merits regardless of its effect upon any private company that wants to get a monopoly in foreign trade or any other sort of trade, aviation, or any other kind. (US Senate, 1945: 111.)

The hearings revealed considerable confusion about the relative status and interconnections of the four documents emanating from the Chicago conference. Attention focussed on the Five Freedoms Agreement. First, the legality of the agreement was questioned. Several senators, including

Bailey, who had been a delegate at Chicago, pointed out that the Civil Aeronautics Act of 1938 prescribed CAB permits for access to American gateways by foreign airlines. The Five Freedoms Agreement, on the contrary, granted concessions automatically (cf. Smith, 1950: 200).

Furthermore, critics in the Senate claimed that the United States would be giving up more than it was gaining by granting fifth-freedom privileges multilaterally. Hawaii, 'the key to the Pacific,' was a particularly sore point. Said Senator Brewster:

We are giving that key away before our boys have even got it secured, allowing any country that signs this agreement a formal authorization to have it, which means Spain or Argentina or any other country with which we make this agreement to have those rights; and I view that with terrific concern in view of what has heretofore transpired; so I have felt so strongly that these matters should be subject to bilateral approach with countries in which we might have confidence. (US Senate, 1945: 65.)

Disapproval of the Five Freedoms Agreement continued to block ratification of the Convention. This treaty had to be ratified by twenty-six nations before becoming effective. As the leading aviation nation, the United States was expected to set an example to others by early ratification. The delay was an embarrassment to the President and the State Department. Only after President Truman sent a special message to the Senate in June 1946, and the State Department made a strategic retreat by announcing US withdrawal from the Five Freedoms Agreement in the following month, did the Senate finally ratify the Convention (Smith, 1950: 322–3).

British opinion was divided as well. Whereas the House of Lords accepted the results of the Chicago conference, the House of Commons was more critical. Yet 'resentment was directed more at the United States than at Lord Swinton' (Smith, 1950: 194). The British press, however, was in general critical of the accomplishments at Chicago. The laborite *Daily Herald* characterized the conference as a 'melancholy failure'; the *Daily Mail* claimed that the failure was due to the lack of a concerted Commonwealth approach; and a BBC com-

*[handwritten margin note at top: Question is: Why did Lab Party alter policy when in govt? If negotiation, & ∴ freedom to decern, is central to regimes this should not be so.]*

mentator called the outcome of the negotiations at Chicago 'an amicable agreement to disagree' (Smith, 1950: 194–5).

The mid-1945 general election in Britain resulted in a Labour victory. The new government announced its aviation policy in a White Paper of December 1945. While repeating the party's commitment to an internationalist regime, the paper conceded that the nations 'are not yet prepared to place their air services under the control of a single international owning and operating body and there is insufficient support to make possible the formation of such bodies on a regional basis.' As the Chicago conference had failed to achieve 'a plan of orderly development in the air,' the government would strive to negotiate bilateral agreements with other countries to 'facilitate the later establishment of a multilateral Convention based on order in the air' (Cooper, 1968: 404).

*[handwritten margin note: but this is again ct Lab. policy quoted earlier. Power makes a difference]*

Thus, while internal debates raged in both Britain and the United States as to whether the Chicago conference was a success or a failure, bilateral diplomacy replaced multilateralism at the international level. First, the United States and Britain sought allies for their own campaigns; 'throughout the world both countries worked frantically to win friends so as to block the aspirations of rivals' (Smith, 1950: 247). In several countries lying athwart essential long-haul routes American and British interests clashed. Many of these countries belonged, or had belonged, to the British empire which was exploited to the full by the British. The Americans, on the other hand, could capitalize on their aircraft production and know-how in this 'world sparring match between the two nations.'

All over the world British and American operators snarled at each other. The two governments worked to keep foreign rivals from their spheres of influence. Wherever one country had friends in power, the other was driven from the air. Great Britain and the United States were like rival gangsters. Each had its 'mob' and its respective 'patch,' where it was unsafe for others to venture. (Smith, 1950: 254–5.)

A direct confrontation between the two occurred in late 1945 over New York-London fares (Smith, 1950: 251–4). Finally, in early 1946 British and American representatives agreed to meet at Bermuda in an effort to settle the air quarrels which threatened to create a breach between two old allies. Despite low initial expectations, the two delegations managed to reach a compromise agreement. The timing of the bilateral talks was significant. The British balance of payments was in a crisis, and the British were simultaneously negotiating to obtain a $3.75 billion loan from the United States on easy terms — a circumstance which aided the Americans in extracting British concessions in the field of air transport (Thornton, 1970: 35). Stokeley Morgan of the US delegation at Bermuda (quoted in Smith, 1950: 258) has testified to the American use of issue linkage in the negotiations:

During the few months before the Bermuda Conference the State Department had been urgently pressing the British for this meeting. It had been subtly pointed out that the bad effect it would have on the British loan negotiations if a strong effort to reach some agreement were not made before the loan came up for debate in the Senate. It was no secret that the airlines lobby would work against the British loan if our aviation interests continued to be ignored.

The Americans had put additional pressure on the British by concluding a bilateral agreement with Eire in early 1945 without consulting the British beforehand. Eire controlled the important transit point of Shannon on the edge of the Atlantic. In response to Churchill's resentment, Roosevelt warned that 'aviation circles in this country are becoming increasingly suspicious that certain elements in England intend to try to block the development of international flying in general until the British aviation industry is further developed' (quoted in Sampson, 1985: 90–1).

When the American and British negotiators met at Bermuda in January 1946 their respective positions were far apart; yet in six weeks they succeeded in reaching an agreement. In informal contacts prior to the Bermuda meeting both sides had signaled their willingness to make concessions without specifying in which areas (Smith, 1950: 258). The compromise that emerged at Bermuda resulted from an exchange of concessions. The United States gave up its previous resistance to controlling rates and fares, while

Britain abandoned its demand for predetermination of the frequency and capacity to be operated by each airline (Wheatcroft, 1964: 71). Thus the Americans were able to acquire fifth-freedom traffic rights and the extra frequencies so long demanded, at the same time as the British won a US commitment against cut-throat competition (Smith, 1950: 258).

The American acceptance of the right of IATA to set rates, subject to government approval, came as a pleasant surprise to the British. It had not been advertised before the Bermuda meeting. In the words of one American negotiator, 'if the British had known they were going to get their own way on rates, they would have been twice as tough on frequencies' (Stokeley Morgan, quoted in Smith, 1950: 258).

Yet there were previous indications that such an American concession could be expected. First, tariff regulation had been a central feature of American domestic air transport since 1938 (Wheatcroft, 1964: 75). Furthermore, an interdepartmental working committee had recommended in April 1943 that 'to avoid destructive competition, a generalized agreement should provide for the creation of a regular "conference" to set rates, analogous to the shipping "conferences" which set the "conference rates" for ocean passenger and freight service' (Berle, 1973: 482-3). And at Chicago the chief US negotiator, Adolf Berle, had spoken favorably of minimum rate agreements by operator conferences (US Department of State, 1948: 447-8).

Similarly, there had been forebodings of Britain's concession on frequency. In the secret tripartite talks at Chicago, the British at one point gave up their 'escalation' scheme. Adolf Berle reported to Washington that 'the British re-examined their position' and 'really abandoned it'; he characterized this as 'the real "break" in the Conference' (Berle, 1973: 500-1). The British concession was obviously the result of bad communications between London and the delegation at Chicago (Sampson, 1985: 85), and the British negotiators subsequently had to revert and cover up. All the same, the incident had revealed a weak spot in the British armor.

In view of the acrimonious exchanges at Chicago only a year earlier, the US-British Bermuda compromise may seem surprising. However, both countries, as we have seen, were under heavy pressure to reach an agreement. Moreover, there was not the same clash of personalities as at Chicago; in fact, the negotiating teams were new on both sides. One observer (Smith, 1950: 257) attributes much of the success at Bermuda to the negotiators: 'Here, again, something had been learned since the Chicago days. The British were careful to select spokesmen who could face new ideas without rancor. The U.S. delegation was much more unified than it had been at Chicago.'

The American negotiating team consisted of military experts, airline managers and officials of the CAB and the State Department (Thayer, 1965: 77). This broad representation in the negotiations did not prevent internal disagreements as to the value of the eventual result.

Pan American was opposed to the Bermuda agreement. Two influential members of the Senate, Owen Brewster and Pat McCarran, complained that the United States had come out second best — whereas Britain under the agreement would increase its route mileage from 29,000 to 109,000 miles, the United States had gained only 57,000 miles — and argued that the British should therefore be given harsher treatment on the terms of their $3.75 billion loan (Smith, 1950: 262; Thornton, 1970: 38). And whereas CAB Chairman Welch Pogue defended the agreement, a minority within the Board maintained that fare-setting by IATA was 'the antithesis of a competitive system' (Smith, 1950: 261). The seeds were thus sown for a perennial controversy within the US aviation community.

## Conclusions

The negotiators at Chicago in 1944, unlike their counterparts at Paris in 1919, acted from divergent perceptions. Stemming from different historical experiences, asymmetric issue-specific power, and dissimilar interests in postwar aviation, these divergent perceptions led the chief protagonists to suspect each other of ulterior motives. In the words of C.D. Howe, the leader of the Canadian delegation at Chicago, 'many of the difficulties arose from misconceptions' (US Department of State, 1948: 69). Most countries, having escaped the United States' traumatic experiences with monopolies and trusts, failed to see airline cooperation as dangerous, harmful or undesirable. The United States, on the other hand, conditioned by its liberal ethos to equate harmony and cooperation domestically as well as internationally with free enterprise and free trade, looked askance at foreign charges of imperialism.

Unlike in 1919, the bargaining process in the wake of World War II eventually ushered in a compromise between divergent positions. The bargaining process differed from the Paris peace conference, insofar as it was quite lengthy — from the initial contacts to the final Bermuda agreement some two years elapsed, whereas the Paris convention was negotiated in less than two months. Nor were the negotiations after World War II facilitated by a pre-existing informal network as in 1919. The Chicago conference witnessed a clash of principles, pitting states against each other without the mitigating effect of any intermediary. The efforts of one state, Canada, to act as mediator, though helpful, did not bring about a comprehensive agreement.

The greater number of bargaining parties obviously contributed to the difficulties of reaching an agreement at Chicago. It is significant that the final compromise was the result of bilateral negotiations between the two leading aviation nations, the United States and Britain.

Attempts at coalition-building tended to reinforce the bilateral controversy after World War II, as the United States and Britain strived to recruit supporters of their respective positions. Although there were obvious internal disagreements among the major states, these were not exploited for the building of cross-national coalitions — with the exception of Pan Am's and BOAC's abortive cartel efforts.

There was diffuse issue linkage at Chicago, insofar as the negotiators generally envisaged an aviation agreement as an example of how nations might work out other differences (Smith, 1950: 141). The Canadian representative C.D. Howe expressed it thus:

An enlightened settlement of the problem of international air transport will mean that the nations of the world have gone a long way toward establishing a lasting peace and a new order of security.

Taken with the organization foreshadowed by the Dumbarton Oaks meetings, it would constitute a model for the settlement of other difficult international problems and would create an atmosphere in which the settlement of these other problems will be easier. On the other hand, if we cannot devise a working system of cooperation and collaboration between the nations of the world in the field of air transport, there will be a smaller chance of our enjoying peace for the remainder of our lives. (US Department of State, 1948: 74.)

Specific issue linkage proved to be an effective means of reaching a compromise agreement, as US-British aviation negotiations at Bermuda were explicitly linked with Britain's much-needed loan from the United States.

In brief, knowledge of the preceding bargaining process obviously adds to our understanding of the timing, form and content of the Chicago-Bermuda regime. To be sure, the negotiators at Chicago, unlike their counterparts at Paris in 1919, had several alternative proposals before them. The controversy was essentially bilateral, with the United States and Britain as the chief protagonists. Yet it was never an either/or choice, as assumed by situational explanations; nor was the bargaining process streamlined and linear. In other words, the game metaphor of the situational model does not seem fully applicable. Henry Ladd Smith (1950: 256) has suggested a different metaphor to describe the untidy bargaining process after World War II:

The United States and Great Britain were like two drunks helping each other back to their walk-up apartment, climbing a few steps, wrangling on the landing, wobbling up another flight, fighting again noisily, to the annoyance of the neighbors, but slowly nearing the peacefulness of their destination.

# 7 Attempted regime change in the late 1970s

American attempts at revising the Chicago-Bermuda regime in the late 1970s involved complex bargaining processes among several actors at different levels. Most of these actors were organizational ones. In trying to disentangle the multilevel bargaining processes, let us therefore start by looking at those organizations which constituted parts of a potential international aviation network at the time of the American regime challenge.

## Organizational development after World War II[1]

The Chicago-Bermuda regime bestowed important functions on two international organizations, ICAO and IATA. The intergovernmental organization (IGO) ICAO, a member of the United Nations family, has promoted multilateral cooperation among governments in the technical field of standardizing air navigation practices and equipment. Its immediate concern has been the drafting of international standards and recommended practices. Besides, ICAO is a forum-type organization where all interested member states and organizations participate in the deliberation of technical issues and webs of relationships among various actors are created (Kihl, 1971: 74).

Though not a creation of the Chicago conference as ICAO, IATA also owes its origin to that international gathering. Immediately following the official discussions at Chicago, a meeting took place between the airline representatives who were present, either as delegates or advisers. They agreed that a worldwide airline organization had to be created as a counterpart to ICAO in order to promote the views and needs of the airlines. At an airline conference in Havana in April 1945 the International Air Transport Association was established. While inheriting the acronym of the interwar International Air Traffic Association, the new IATA had no legal connection with the old association, which was officially abolished at a meeting in London in September 1945 (Brancker, 1977: 9–10).

Because of the crucial fare-setting function bestowed on IATA in the 1946 Bermuda agreement, this nongovernmental organization (NGO) was elevated to center stage and soon became 'the central focus of the system' (Thornton, 1971: 198). In addition to fare coordination, inter-airline cooperation within IATA has produced a unique global transportation system through a number of measures which can be subsumed under the rubric of 'interlining.'

Since no single airline offers service to each and every point, worldwide mobility by air is only made possible by transfers between airlines. The welding of individual airline systems has encompassed building a global scheduling, reservations and communication system, standardizing tickets and carrier/location codes, and coordinating airport handling of passengers, cargo and mail. The IATA Clearing House, established in 1947, facilitates financial settlement of transactions between participating airlines; and the IATA Prorate Agency, established in 1951, administers the division (proration) of through fares involving two or more airlines. The multilateral interline system allows passengers to make reservations and arrange a single ticket with one airline or agent for any number of airlines, flights, connections, stopovers, etc.; to pay for the ticket in a single currency; to change the booking to a different airline without re-issuance of ticket, or to change the itinerary *en route*; and to through-check the baggage to each stopover point irrespective of the number of airlines or connecting points (cf. Brancker, 1977: 45–58; IATA, 1980).

At its first annual meeting in October 1945, IATA had a membership of forty-two airlines (Brancker, 1977: 10). By the late 1970s IATA had evolved into an organization of some 120 international airlines. About three-quarters of these airlines were wholly or predominantly government-owned. Through the airlines IATA thus had important indirect links with

individual governments — the organization has, in fact,
frequently been characterized as 'quasi-governmental' (see,
e.g., Chuang, 1972).

Moreover, IATA maintains regular contacts with some
seventy international organizations and agencies. The link
with ICAO is considered especially important. IATA and
ICAO have observer status in each other's organization, and
IATA is a 'very active observer,' to quote one IATA official.
The wording of IATA working papers often finds its way to
ICAO resolutions via airlines and governments. ICAO officials confirm that IATA has a 'privileged position' within
ICAO, being able to participate and table documents in all
committees and panels. At the same time, they lament the
lack of reciprocity: ICAO participates in just a few of the IATA
forums, and then strictly as observers. Whereas IATA is
active in the technical field as well and represents the views
of the airlines to ICAO and individual governments, ICAO
had little or no say in fare-setting or other economic matters
up to the late 1970s. At any rate, members of the IATA and
ICAO Secretariats alike testify to their mutual working
relations and close interaction.

The regional level displays a similar dualistic pattern. A
number of regional airline associations have been created —
sometimes out of discontent with IATA. Though not sub-
ordinate regional organizations of IATA, these associations
interact frequently with IATA as well as with their regional
IGO counterparts (cf. Table 1). Hence IATA maintains links
with national governments at the regional level as well.

**Table 1.** Regional aviation NGOs and IGOs

| *NGOs* | *IGOs* |
|---|---|
| AFRAA (African Airlines Association) | AFCAC (African Civil Aviation Commission) |
| AEA (Association of European Airlines) | ECAC (European Civil Aviation Conference) |
| AACO (Arab Air Carriers Organization) | ACAC (Arab Civil Aviation Council) |
| AITAL (Asociacion International de Transporte Aereo Latinoamericano) | LACAC (Latin American Civil Aviation Conference) |

The diversification of actors often recurs on domestic levels. This was especially true of the United States in the late 1970s, where decision-making on international aviation matters typically involved a host of organizational actors. The Civil Aeronautics Board (CAB) was an independent regulatory commission licensing and designating airlines, regulating fares and determining standards of service and equipment. The Departments of Transportation, State and Justice followed international aviation developments closely. The White House and Congress occasionally got involved. Inter-agency groups had been created to coordinate policy among the various governmental actors. Among several pressure groups, the organization of American regular carriers, the Air Transport Association (ATA) held a prominent position.

In short, in the decades following the creation of the Chicago-Bermuda regime a potential international aviation network had evolved with multiple links facilitating communication and coalition-building across national borders. In the following we shall see to what extent and in what ways this network was mobilized when the Chicago-Bermuda regime came under attack in the late 1970s.

## The American challenge in the late 1970s: Renegotiating bilateral agreements

As we have seen, the US challenge to the Chicago-Bermuda regime after 1977 consisted of denunciation and renegotiation of several *bilateral* agreements, on the one hand, and an attack on the *multilateral* fare-setting framework, on the other. The latter aspect represented the most serious challenge to the existing international regime, and my subsequent analysis will focus on the multilevel bargaining process triggered by the so-called Show Cause Order. However, a brief description of US objectives and strategies in renegotiating its bilateral agreements in the late 1970s and early 1980s is warranted.

The bilateral US-British Bermuda agreement of 1946 developed into a 'quasi-multilateral structure' (Harbison, 1982: 45), insofar as the Bermuda principles came to serve as models for other bilateral agreements around the world. Similarly, the United States used bilateral negotiations in the late 1970s in an attempt to establish certain principles of international aviation.

The US objectives were spelled out in a policy document of 21 August 1978 (White House, 1978), which built on — but in several respects differed significantly from — a draft released for comment on 23 May. In forthcoming bilateral negotiations the United States was to promote 'new and greater opportunities for innovative and competitive pricing,' 'liberalization of charter rules,' 'elimination of restrictions on capacity, frequency, and route and operating rights,' and 'flexibility to designate multiple U.S. airlines in international air markets.' The 1978 policy document elaborated the new US pricing policy:

The U.S. will develop new bilateral procedures to encourage a more competitive system for establishing scheduled air fares and rates. Charter pricing must continue to be competitive. Fares, rates and prices should be determined by individual airlines based primarily on competitive considerations in the marketplace.

With respect to charters the document argued:

The introduction of charters acted as a major catalyst to the expansion of international air transportation in the 1960's. Charters are a competitive spur and exert downward pressure on the pricing of scheduled services. Charters generate new traffic and help stimulate expansion in all sectors of the industry. Restrictions which have been imposed on the volume, frequency, and regularity of charter services as well as requirements for approval of individual charter flights have restrained the growth of traffic and tourism and do not serve the interests of either party to an aviation agreement. Strong efforts will be made to obtain liberal charter provisions in bilateral agreements.

The document was less explicit on the negotiating methods to be used to achieve these objectives, merely stating:

We will aggressively pursue our interests in expanded air transportation and reduced prices rather than accept the self-defeating accommodation of protectionism. Our concessions in negotiations will be given in return for progress toward competitive objectives, and these concessions themselves will be of a liberalizing character.

As would soon become evident, the US negotiating strategy consisted of a carrot-and-stick approach which could be labelled 'routes for rates' (Harbison, 1982: 45). In return for concessions to the American demands for competitive pricing and liberalized capacity and charter provisions, the United States offered the carrot of new route access to valuable US markets for foreign carriers.

The stick was represented by threats of traffic diversion. On the North Atlantic, for example, the geography of Europe makes each country capable of diverting traffic from its neighbors by offering lower prices. And US carriers could easily substitute one European gateway for another. Reluctant adversaries in bilateral negotiations with the United States could thus risk the erosion of 'their' traffic to other routes (cf. Harbison, 1982: 51).

Tactics of geographical leverage were central to this negotiating strategy. Already by October 1977, CAB Chairman Alfred Kahn had recommended in an interview that the United States should 'canvass the world, select out the potential partners offering them the most promising of opportunities, and actively seek out negotiations with them on a bilateral or multilateral basis' (quoted in Harbison, 1982: 45). In Europe, Belgium and the Netherlands were logical candidates. In November 1977, a new bilateral agreement with Belgium was concluded which, despite its vague and basically hortative wording, was heralded as the new US model text to replace the restrictive Bermuda II agreement with Britain. And in March 1978, a US-Dutch agreement introduced country-of-origin rules to scheduled air services (Harbison, 1982: 149–51).

The agreements with Belgium and the Netherlands were designed to put pressure on the British.

It was not mere coincidence, I assure you, that we concluded the agreement with the Dutch — with their acceptance of country-of-origin rules not just for charters but also for pricing of scheduled services — right in the middle of our negotiations with the British, and it was not mere coincidence either that almost immediately after announcement of that agreement, the British decided to accept the prices we had approved for scheduled service between our two countries as well. (Kahn, 1978.)

Britain did make certain *ad hoc* concessions to the US position on pricing after skirmishes, where the British disapproved Braniff's proposed Dallas/Fort Worth-London fares and the US CAB threatened retaliation against British Caledonian. Yet the formal framework of Bermuda II remained intact (Harbison, 1982: 188–91).

The continued use of geographical leverage tactics was discussed with unusual candor in an internal CAB memorandum of 26 February 1979, which became publicly known through a conscious or accidental leak (Levine, 1979). Written by one of the most influential members of the CAB staff, Michael Levine, the document pointed to Europe as the primary target of US efforts to denounce existing bilateral agreements:

There is political merit in the argument advanced by the DOS [Department of State] that the U.S. might be successfully charged with racism or imperialism if the first bilateral the U.S. denounces is with a country without a predominantly European background or one which is very much less economically developed than we are. If we first denounced an agreement with one of our European brethren, other nations more remotely related to the U.S. should correctly interpret this as a signal that the U.S. is now willing to denounce bilateral civil aviation agreements. The symbolism of this first act, of and in itself, should be helpful to other negotiations in progress in other parts of the globe, especially Japan.

Levine's memorandum pointed to Spain, Portugal, Greece and possibly Yugoslavia as 'the most promising short-term innovative agreement partners in Europe.' Liberal agreements with these countries 'would put the most short-term traffic pressure on both France and Italy.' Neither the French nor the Italians were deemed likely to yield to the American competitive position in direct bilateral negotiations; only increased market pressure would make them surrender.

Since Italy is the fourth largest European market for American travel, it should be increasingly affected by more liberal charters and scheduled prices available through other gateways. ... As with Italy, we think that *bona fide* 'diversion' of France-destined traffic to other gateways is the only means toward a procompetitive agreement with the French.

The American negotiation offensive met with only limited success. Several important aviation nations — such as Britain, France, Italy and Japan — failed to yield to US pressure. By the end of 1982 the Americans had managed to conclude only some twenty 'liberal' bilateral agreements (Harbison, 1982: 12).

The US negotiating strategy met with resistance at home as well. American international carriers — especially Pan Am and TWA, the traditional 'flag carriers' — voiced their dissatisfaction with the new 'liberal' agreements which they felt were working to their disadvantage. Willis Player, a retired Pan Am executive, publicly stated:

We hate to see our government giving away real, hard, intrinsic, measurable values — our geography, if you will — for value that is only nominal at worst and short-term at best. We're competing in a world that does not exist the way these instant experts think it exists. We're not corporations competing on an equal footing with other corporations. We're competing with other governments that have firm, consistent, and mostly protective aviation policies. (*Business Week*, 1981: 41.)

Pan Am Chairman William Seawell amplified this theme in a letter to CAB Chairman Marvin Cohen:

Pan Am was an early and ardent supporter of domestic deregulation, and internationally we are fully ready, willing and able to face all competition that a free marketplace can support. However, we believe that the policies of the past four years have failed to recognize the inequities of the international marketplace, and that these policies have given foreign carriers a decided competitive advantage. We further believe that this unequal treatment has played a major role in compounding the serious financial problems being faced not only by Pan Am, but also by the U.S. international industry in general. (Seawell, 1981.)

The original Bermuda principles, requiring the approval of each affected government before a service could be operated, made explicit the power of each government to disapprove any tariff proposed to or from its territory. In pressing for 'liberal' bilateral agreements, the United States sought to reverse this equation and make government disapproval virtually impossible (cf. Harbison, 1982: 212). This new principle gained no universal acceptance or following; the overwhelming majority of bilateral agreements in the aviation world remain based upon the Bermuda principles.

US policy and the liberal agreements are, in regulatory terms, the cuckoo in the nest. They represent an aggressively different minority in what is otherwise a homogeneous bilateral network. Out of a probable 2000 air transport bilateral arrangements and formal agreements governing international routes, the liberal agreements account for some 20. (Harbison, 1982: 207.)

## The Show Cause Order[2]

If a CAB initiative was expected by mid-1978, the kind of action taken came as a surprise. The unprecedented and unfamiliar 'show cause' procedure was the result of a CAB staff initiative. No prior consultations were made with the Department of State (DOS) or Department of Transportation (DOT). And the Board adopted the order 'almost casually' without much background analysis, as evidenced by the subsequently released transcript of its non-public meeting (Rein & McDonald, 1982: 237–8).

The CAB order initiated a judicial process in which all interaction had to be through attorneys and informal contacts with the CAB at any level were precluded by law. Moreover, the SCO was a proceeding which, unlike other types of CAB orders, was not subject to presidential review (Haanappel, 1983: 163). The harsh language and unilateral nature of the order created a confrontational setting both domestically and internationally.

Domestically, the SCO added fuel to an ongoing power struggle between the CAB, DOS and DOT. At the time of the order, the CAB and DOS were allied in opposing DOT's attempts to assume a leadership role in international aviation matters. As we shall see, this coalition pattern would eventually be modified by the SCO.

The novel CAB initiative caused bewilderment at home and abroad.

Neither the Federal Aviation Act nor the CAB regulations contain rules defining circumstances under which show cause orders may appropriately be used. Nor did CAB precedent provide guidance to potentially interested parties concerning how the proceeding would evolve, or the rights to which they were entitled. (Rein & McDonald, 1982: 239.)

The immediate target of the SCO, IATA was probably the first actor to realize the implications of the order. The first choice IATA had to make was whether to take an active part in the SCO proceedings or stay on the sideline. This issue, in fact, caused acrimonious intra-Secretariat discussions. Members of the legal department initially recommended 'diplomatic aloofness' on the part of IATA, leaving any intervention to individual carriers and/or governments. The main reasons why the Secretariat should restrain its activity to a bare minimum, in their view, were (a) that an active IATA stance would confirm the 'cartel' image subscribed to by the CAB, and (b) that the lack of inter-carrier consensus made it impossible for IATA to act as spokesman for the entire industry. The prevalent view in the Office of the Director General, on the other hand, was that an IATA response to the SCO was essential and that the Secretariat, rather than rely on spontaneous external reactions, ought to plan for active coordination of airline and government reaction.

These internal divisions of opinion notwithstanding, the Director General (DG) took the initiative in securing a mandate from the members for an active IATA posture. On 29 June IATA's Executive Committee (ExCom) authorized the DG to (a) bring the SCO to the attention of member airlines; (b) prepare background material for airlines to use with their governments; and (c) prepare a 'possible' IATA submission to the CAB. The IATA Secretariat had thus received a mandate for active involvement and now turned to considerations of strategy and tactics *vis-à-vis* other actors in the international aviation community.

The IATA Secretariat from the outset assessed the Show Cause Order as primarily a political issue. In a memo to the ExCom, the Director General pointed out that the CAB had raised 'questions of principle which are fundamentally political in nature.' IATA's Washington counsel depicted the SCO as a '90 percent political, 10 percent legal' issue. National governments were thus seen as the key actors in the political process initiated by the SCO. Moreover, IATA officials were keenly aware that governments had to be convinced that their self-interest — not only IATA's existence — was at stake.

Another basic premise of the IATA Secretariat's policy discussions was the realization that the US aviation community was far from monolithic. The DOS and the DOT were perceived to be more susceptible to IATA arguments than the CAB. Furthermore, it was well recognized that the CAB was divided. One Board member, Richard O'Melia, had in fact gone on record with his dissenting opinion of the SCO: 'first, the show cause order sets forth tentative findings and conclusions which I cannot at this time endorse, and, secondly, there is an arbitrary and unilateral tone in the measure that I do not subscribe to, which is unnecessary and certain to cause irritation and resentment among foreign government authorities' (CAB, 1978). The possibility of capitalizing on such internal US differences of opinion was therefore a central component of all IATA strategy discussions.

The conclusion the IATA Secretariat drew from these premises was to focus on certain links in the international aviation network, especially the governments-DOS-CAB link, in its efforts to influence the SCO proceedings. The calculation was that unless enough governments were to voice their misgivings about the SCO to the US Department of State, the DOS was unlikely to take spontaneous action *vis-à-vis* the CAB. Obviously the first question, then, was how to reach and alert national governments.

The IATA Secretariat primarily utilized the link with national governments through individual carriers and regional carrier organizations. Member airlines were asked to appoint special Show Cause contacts who were virtually bombarded with SCO information through letters, telexes, phone calls, and face-to-face communications. The bottom line of these messages was consistently a call for carrier action urging their respective foreign ministries in their own interest to make *démarches* to the US Department of State. On the basis of available information from Washington, it was obvious to the IATA Secretariat that such government representations should be made at the political level of the DOS, not only to its aviation or economic affairs specialists.

The US carriers, primary targets of the CAB action, were divided on the SCO issue. Pan Am and TWA, the principal international carriers, supported IATA; other carriers favored international deregulation for tactical reasons, to court favor with the CAB and obtain new international routes; and only a few airlines supported the CAB action out of conviction. Because of the vulnerable position of the US carriers *vis-à-vis* the CAB, the IATA Secretariat decided to concentrate its efforts on non-American airlines while maintaining broad, general liaison with US carriers and ATA, the trade association of American airlines.

Although the European airlines were most directly affected by the SCO, the IATA Secretariat estimated that the US government might be equally sensitive to the concerns of weaker Third World carriers and governments. Therefore a major effort was made to inform and involve African, Asian and Latin American actors. This, however, was far from unproblematic.

First, IATA soon ran into difficulties in trying to persuade small carriers not serving the United States of the necessity of a response to the SCO. Even among large carriers serving the United States there was less than complete understanding of the implications of US antitrust laws for the carriers and their home governments. Therefore, IATA's Washington counsel was instructed to prepare a hard-hitting analysis of the international implications of US antitrust laws. Completed in September 1978, the study demonstrated that these laws can be — and have in fact been — applied to commercial activities outside the United States, and that the penalties were substantial.

Non-IATA carriers represented a problem, particularly in Asia where several major flag carriers remained outside IATA. Here IATA's Regional Director formed a link with the non-IATA carriers through the Orient Airlines Association (OAA) which grouped both IATA and non-IATA members.

This example indicates that, in addition to carriers, a number of international organizations were utilized by the IATA Secretariat as channels to inform national governments and thus induce them to react to the SCO. Foremost among these were regional aviation organizations, both NGOs and IGOs. The primary targets were the regional carrier organizations, but regional aviation IGOs were also approached directly.

ICAO became part of the mobilized network as well. Since 1971 some ICAO member states, especially those attracting tourism, had made efforts to initiate greater ICAO involvement in international fare setting. These matters were considered 'far too important to be left to airlines alone,' to quote the delegate of Barbados (ICAO, 1971: 58). Such proposals were opposed by other states, who considered the existing system adequate, and by members of the ICAO Secretariat, who did not want the additional work associated with a widened role for ICAO. Yet, as a compromise, ICAO in 1974 established a small expert panel on fares and rates. While originally inspired by anti-IATA sentiments, the installment of the fare-setting issue on the ICAO agenda eventually came to work to the advantage of IATA.

In 1977 ICAO convened a Special Air Transport Conference, to which IATA sent thirty observers. The emerging shift in US aviation policy cast its shadow on the conference. On the initiative of ICAO's expert panel on fares and rates, the conference adopted a recommendation urging greater government involvement in international fare setting (ICAO, 1977: 27). At the same time, another recommendation, obliquely aimed at US aviation policy, was adopted: 'Unilateral action by governments which may have a negative effect on carriers' efforts towards reaching agreement should be avoided as far as possible' (ICAO, 1977: 25). The wording of this recommendation coincided in large measure with an IATA working paper presented at the outset of the conference.

The CAB Show Cause Order appeared to be an example of the kind of unilateral government action stigmatized in the 1977 ICAO recommendation. When the SCO issue was brought before the ICAO Council in late 1978, there was little knowledge of its implications among the Council members. However, IATA representatives were quite active in 'filling the knowledge gap,' to use the expression of one interviewed ICAO official. Through its Air Transport Director in Montreal, IATA could also approach Council members whose airlines were not members of IATA and who were therefore more difficult to reach. In December 1978, the ICAO Council did, in fact, adopt a resolution requesting member states to 'refrain from any unilateral action which would endanger multilateral fares and rates setting systems' (ICAO, 1978a: 131).

Although the indirect links to national governments and to the US Department of State were assigned top priority by the IATA Secretariat, direct approaches were made as well. Links were established, especially between IATA's Regional Directors and national civil aviation authorities and transportation ministries, where the IATA representatives, according to an internal memo, argued that 'all their enthusiasm will come to nothing if, in addition to their action with CAB, political action was not taken.' IATA representatives were frequently present at regional meetings of civil aviation authorities to state their SCO case in formal presentations and off-the-floor discussions.

Similarly, IATA maintained direct ties with the US Department of State. Members of the IATA Secretariat had an informal meeting with high DOS officials in August 1978, and in early January 1979 the DG met with Richard Cooper, Under-Secretary for Economic Affairs in Washington. Later that same month a symposium on international aviation policy in Kingston, Jamaica, organized by the DOS, ended in confrontation between IATA and foreign carrier representatives, on the one hand, and the DOS, on the other. According to DOS respondents, this confrontation played an important role in sensitizing the DOS to the explosive nature of the SCO issue.

In brief, the IATA Secretariat considered action by national governments with the US Department of State key to an eventual reversal of the CAB's tentative finding calling the very existence of IATA into question. In a concerted effort to influence the key actors, the IATA Secretariat relied primarily on indirect links via carriers and carrier organizations but also exploited other, subsidiary channels, including direct access to governments and the DOS. The network thus mobilized is represented graphically in Figure 9.

Whereas these circuitous influence attempts were pivotal in IATA's strategy, efforts were also made at direct leverage

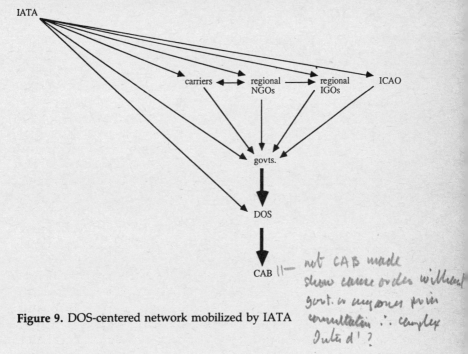

**Figure 9.** DOS-centered network mobilized by IATA

on the CAB. Based on the perception that the CAB was not susceptible to logical argumentation and was not likely to judge the matter on its merits, one basic IATA strategy *vis-à-vis* the CAB was an 'all-fronts attack to get proceedings slowed down.' The deferral of all procedural dates was considered to be in IATA's interest, since 'so long as the Board does not act, the pre-existing approval of IATA rate machinery remains in force.' Thus, the IATA Secretariat's principal strategy was 'to avoid any setting in motion of decision machinery,' whereas efforts 'to achieve a favorable, or neutral, CAB result' were labelled a 'secondary strategy.'

Although the chances of persuading the CAB were not deemed great, IATA put considerable work into drafting its own submission to the CAB in response to the SCO and persuading its member carriers to make similar submissions. The drafting of IATA's response started as early as July; in mid-September a draft was presented to the ExCom; and the final IATA submission was filed on 19 December 1978. Already one month earlier, the DG had notified all member airlines of the forthcoming IATA submission, asking them to submit their endorsement or additional arguments to the CAB. The carriers were encouraged to make their views known to the CAB through several 'chaser' telexes, letters and phone calls.

Though originally deemed less important than the Department of State, the US Department of Transportation was also seen by the IATA Secretariat as a possible channel to influence the CAB. The strategy was to spell out the negative implications of the SCO and demonstrate that it would threaten the DOT's role as leadership agency in the formulation of US aviation policy. Members of the IATA Secretariat — including the DG— had private meetings with leading DOT officials on several occasions. The DOT was apparently a receptive target. Former DOT officials have testified in interviews that they sought collaboration with IATA in the early stages of the SCO in trying to understand the complex issue, developing a relationship which at times became 'too cozy.'

Another U.S. government agency which was involved in the SCO issue and which might offer a channel to the CAB was the Department of Justice. However, the IATA Secretariat never entertained any hopes of influencing this agency which was considered 'basically hostile to rate agreements' while holding the antitrust banner high.

The US Congress constituted a significant parallel arena in the SCO proceedings. On 1 August 1978, a new international aviation bill (the so-called Cannon-Pearson Bill) was introduced in the Senate, which, *inter alia*, would prohibit the CAB from approving inter-carrier fare agreements. IATA Director General Knut Hammarskjöld testified before the Senate Commerce Committee in late August and subsequently wrote a letter to Senator Howard Cannon in which he recommended elimination of the section prohibiting inter-carrier fare agreements.

To summarize, IATA's attempts to influence the CAB directly — without using national governments and the US Department of State as intermediaries — aimed at persuading the Board either to defer the SCO proceedings or, less likely, to change its provisional finding. The Secretariat focussed on

IATA and carrier submissions but also utilized regional NGOs and IGOs as well as the US DOT and Congress as channels. A CAB-centered mobilized network can thus be discerned (Figure 10).

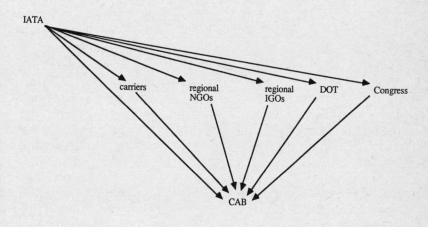

**Figure 10.** CAB-centered network mobilized by IATA

As we have seen, both the DOS and the CAB received an overwhelming amount of submissions supportive of IATA, and the CAB backed down considerably in May by tentatively approving the 'new IATA' and limiting the scope of the SCO proceedings. How influential were IATA's mobilization efforts in shaping this development? No definitive answer can be given to this question, but a few indicators are worth noting.

First, the intensity and volume of IATA's activity must be noted. Member airlines, IATA's principal links with other parts of the international aviation networks, were subjected to a virtual barrage of information and persuasion concerning the Show Cause Order. IATA's leverage was often facilitated by the initially low level of information of carriers and other actors.

It was, however, not merely a question of IATA pressing information upon reluctant recipients; in many cases other actors approached IATA for information. In addition, IATA continuously solicited and obtained information from carriers and other actors concerning planned and implemented SCO actions. Many carriers turned to the IATA Secretariat for assistance in relation to their own submissions to the CAB and so that they could assist their governments in preparing responses to the DOS. IATA thus came to act as a 'clearing-house' for SCO information.

IATA could claim to have been reasonably successful in its multifaceted efforts to mobilize the international aviation network in the early stage of the SCO proceedings. At a June 1979 meeting of SCO contacts in Geneva, one senior IATA official stated:

IATA has made substantial progress in persuading the Board that a multilateral, broad-based airline co-ordinating organization can serve the public interest outside the rate area and in sensitizing the Board to the foreign relations implications of its unilateral attack on IATA rate co-ordination.

Moreover, my interviews indicate that the US aviation community, though well aware that IATA was active on the SCO issue, probably did not realize the full extent of IATA's mobilization and coordination of the international aviation network. Yet in preparation for the impending inter-governmental consultations and the legislative hearings scheduled for late October, the IATA Secretariat increasingly came to rely on direct, rather than indirect, links with governments and US government agencies.

Prior to the regional consultations, IATA officials — in particular the Regional Directors — interacted directly with key government officials. In addition to informal discussions with national civil aviation authorities, IATA officials were invited to be present, for example, at the three regional consultations held — in Bogota, Brussels and Nairobi — as observers. In reality, their role went beyond that of a mere observer. At Bogota and Nairobi pre-caucus IATA observers gave background information of the SCO to the delegates, who were in many cases insufficiently familiar with the subject at issue.

The atmosphere at Bogota was confrontational, and acrimonious exchanges with CAB member Michael Levine led to an abrupt ending of the meeting. At Brussels the European governments were active and aggressive, tabling guidelines for an international agreement on rate coordination which the United States did not accept. Also at Nairobi the US government encountered hostile reactions to its international aviation policy.

The US Department of State was obviously in a delicate position. After some reshuffles in the transportation branch of the DOS, the Under-Secretary for Economic Affairs, Richard Cooper, admitted to *Aviation Daily* on 6 September that the CAB was 'outstaging' the DOS and that 'there was no coordination at all' by the US government on the SCO issue. However, he maintained that the internal disagreements concerned tactics only, whereas there was wide agreement on the objectives of US aviation policy.

At the same time as it concentrated on the inter-governmental consultations via national governments and the DOS, the IATA Secretariat had to plan for direct pressure on the CAB in the legislative hearings. As pointed out in the SCO contacts meeting in June, 'while IATA has challenged strongly the propriety of the proposed legislative hearing and will continue to do so to the extent practical, contingency preparations for responding to this process must be set in motion.'

The IATA Secretariat from the outset realized that it 'must plan to make a substantial showing in favor of the traffic conference system' and at the same time 'avoid fitting the Board's "anti-deregulation" stereotype.' More than fifty potential witnesses were approached and provided with IATA background material. In the end, eighteen IATA-sponsored witnesses appeared in the hearings. In addition to four IATA representatives (including the Director General) and five airline executives, these witnesses included two law professors, one professor of economics, a former US ambassador to the OECD, as well as representatives of the Council of Europe, the British Air Transports User Committee, AFRAA, the Paris Airport Board and a consultant firm. The majority of a total of thirty-two witnesses were thus sponsored by IATA. Moreover, a number of 'independent' witnesses gave testimony in support of IATA, including British Airways, Air Canada, Aer Lingus and the DOT.

The odds did indeed seem to be turning in favor of IATA as the hearings opened. Not only had IATA forced the CAB to yield on procedural matters prior to the hearings, the DOS had in its original written testimony requested that further SCO proceedings be suspended, pending multilateral intergovernmental discussions of the result of a one-year testing period of the revised IATA procedures. And the CAB had retreated one step by limiting the scope of the SCO proceedings to traffic to and from the United States.

The hearings themselves, according to an IATA assessment, were successful in 'providing a strong front against the CAB's examination' and 'establishing an effective formal record of support for IATA's machinery.' The argument of the IATA witnesses focussed on what were perceived to be the vulnerabilities of the CAB position: the link between interlining/prorating and tariff coordination, intervening political forces in international aviation, and the unacceptable results of a free market in international as distinct from domestic air transport (for a summary of the arguments used by both sides in the hearings, see Magdalénat, 1980). According to a leading CAB representative, the interlining argument, in particular, made a certain impression on the Board. CAB Chairman Marvin Cohen (1980a) publicly confessed that 'the Board was impressed by the support given by the new IATA mechanism not only by many witnesses who are familiar with the industry, but also by our own Departments of Transportation and State and other foreign government leaders who support the procompetitive policies of the United States.'

Optimism prevailed in the IATA Secretariat after the hearings. 'I must confess a renewed feeling of confidence about the future of international aviation,' wrote Knut Hammarskjöld in his letter of thanks to the IATA witnesses. And a report from IATA's Washington counsel dwelled on the organization's 'increased credibility' in the United States.

This whole affair seems more to do with domestic politics rather than IR!

*Attempted regime change* 139

This optimism was sustained by developments in the US Congress. Knut Hammarskjöld testified and submitted written comments to the Senate Subcommittee on Aviation in August and to the House Subcommittee on Aviation in October on the Cannon-Pearson Bill. The House Bill which was adopted on 13 November was consistent with IATA's recommendations concerning State Department and possible presidential review of CAB decisions on intercarrier agreements as well as antitrust immunity for agreements not involving US carriers.

Therefore, the CAB retreat on 5 December 1979, when it announced in a press release its decision to 'terminate' the SCO proceedings and grant antitrust immunity to IATA rate coordination not involving US carriers, came as no surprise. According to an internal IATA memo, this 'marks an IATA victory in a major battle but does not end the war.' It was believed in the IATA Secretariat that the practical effect of excluding US carriers differed little from general removal of antitrust immunity, insofar as the US carriers constitute some 50 percent of the markets in which they operate. The immediate public IATA reaction to the CAB's move was therefore negative. The DG, in an interview with the press, characterized it as a 'trial balloon' which, in the absence of foreign reactions, might be the 'first step in unilaterally dismantling the whole system of tariff coordination.'

IATA had succeeded in removing the acute threat to its survival as an organization and seemed to be moving from the defensive to the offensive. At the same time, the realization was gaining ground in the IATA Secretariat that eventually some kind of compromise had to be struck with the United States, that a total victory was unattainable. Actually, such notions had been nurtured by some members of the Secretariat ever since the initiation of the SCO process. For example, one early internal memo envisaged fixed rates as ceilings or a band pricing system as possible compromises. As the SCO process entered a new stage after the legislative hearings, conciliatory signals foreshadowing possible compromise solutions along these lines were intermittently issued by IATA, in particular in the speeches made by the Director General. In April 1979, for example, he suggested 'a blending of minimum and maximum levels, providing for a band or range of fares' (Hammarskjöld, 1979).

Despite its negative public posture, the IATA Secretariat immediately realized the possibilities for compromise contained in the CAB press release of 5 December, and the DG recommended the ExCom that it consider adopting a favorable stance toward the conditions outlined by the CAB — 'innovative' fares to and from the United States and CAB observers in IATA Traffic Conferences.

The IATA Secretariat realized that to get the CAB to take 'one more backward step in the SCO is a difficult but not impossible task,' requiring 'the same type of overall strategy and across-the-board effort IATA has employed to date,' although it was recognized that 'we have exhausted ... a certain amount of government patience with this issue.'

Yet government representatives at the Second Air Transport Conference of ICAO in February 1980 adopted a recommendation which was much more explicit than the 1977 denunciation of detrimental unilateral government actions. Now the ICAO conference, after some controversy, recommended that 'international tariffs should be established multilaterally,' that 'the worldwide multilateral machinery of the IATA Traffic Conferences shall, wherever applicable, be adopted as a first choice when establishing international fares and rates,' and that 'carriers should not be discouraged from participation in the machinery' (ICAO, 1980: 35). Again, several IATA representatives participated in the ICAO conference, and the final recommendations on fares and rates bear a striking resemblance to an IATA working paper put before the conference.

The efforts of the IATA Secretariat increasingly came to center on the search for a compromise solution to the remaining issue at stake — North Atlantic traffic. At a Geneva meeting for SCO contacts in early January 1980, carrier representatives expressed the view that their respective governments would prefer multilateral action through ECAC or ICAO to bilateral action, and there was broad consensus that the most appropriate forum would be the impending round of US-Canada-ECAC tripartite meetings. This new focus implied, first, strong emphasis on IATA-government links and, second, efforts at bringing US carriers back into the

IATA fold. High-level discussions with leading US airlines were initiated. IATA's efforts were helped by the fact that the Secretariat learned that the DOT was polling US carriers on their interest in tariff coordination and that the DOS was actively inquiring as to foreign government reactions to the CAB press release.

After the issue of the April 1980 CAB Order, the IATA Secretariat made a coordinated effort to work out a compromise solution and 'sell' it to the interested parties. The project, known inside IATA as the 'new initiative,' came to engage all boundary-role personnel in the Secretariat in a two-year effort at brokerage in the international aviation network.

Catchwords in the gradually refined IATA proposal were: a 'safety-net approach' (a formula which would not constantly expose the carriers to the uncertainty of government approval/disapproval), based on a 'zone of tolerance' (within which governments would agree not to intervene) and 'fare bands' (within which carriers would agree to allow fare competition). Such a proposal was considered to constitute a compromise between pro-regulation and pro-deregulation forces.

The strategic point of departure was that 'the new initiative must be undertaken by governments.' A US-ECAC-Canada declaration of principles was seen as the most preferable format. However, as pointed out in an internal strategy paper,

it is important that IATA not be perceived as telling government officials how to suck eggs. We should be in the posture of planting ideas ... But the development of the initiative must be done by governments.

The same paper saw the CAB as the most problematic actor to approach:

Even if dressed up, the new initiative is likely to be seen by most of the CAB as another IATA ploy ... But the CAB is the ultimate arbiter of the future of IATA; it will be small comfort to find we have persuaded DOS and DOT only to have the CAB close IATA down out of ignorance anything was afoot.

The solution to this dilemma was to ensure that 'ideas reach the CAB from DOS, DOT, or European governments,' and to allow time for the new thinking to percolate.

The IATA Secretariat was relatively optimistic about DOS and DOT interest in the 'new initiative.' IATA officials therefore maintained close contacts with these two departments, offering 'personal views' on a North Atlantic accommodation.

The European side was somewhat more problematic, from IATA's point of view. Among the carriers that were approached, the reaction was positive but equivocal, 'varying from luke warm to moderately warm.' The 'new initiative' was also probed directly with key government officials. As with carriers, there were differences of opinion between governments as to the advisability and timing of the 'new initiative.' At a minimum, there seemed to be agreement on the value of IATA's undertaking a detailed investigation of flexible pricing formulas. In addition to individual countries, the President and Secretary General of ECAC were approached. The IATA Secretariat provided them with background information and working papers and engaged in several face-to-face discussions.

Canada constituted the third pillar on which to build a consensus. Here IATA first used the indirect link via Air Canada executives who agreed to try to interest Canadian government officials and diplomats in acting as a catalyst with the US government. Subsequently, high-level face-to-face contacts were made with Canadian civil aviation authorities who were provided with 'think papers' in the hope that they could play a mediating role between ECAC and the United States.

There were certain encouraging developments on the American side in the fall of 1980 which were seized upon by the IATA Secretariat. In September the United States concluded a bilateral agreement with China which for the first time adopted a fare bands concept. A similar US-Philippines agreement was signed in October. And in November, Boyd Hight, DOS Deputy Assistant Secretary for Transportation and Telecommunications, made a noted speech in which he hinted at the precedent value of these bilaterals in seeking 'ways to institutionalize fare-making which provide enough flexibility for our policies and enough stability for the other government's policies.' Hight called for 'creative pragmatism which looks behind the slogans that intensify problems for hints of the common interest that can resolve them' (Hight, 1980). Copies of this speech were distributed by the IATA Secretariat to all the actors with which it was interacting in the 'new initiative' campaign.

If there appeared to be a plausible degree of support for the ideas entailed in IATA's 'new initiative' among the main actors in the North Atlantic drama, it became equally clear that none of the actors was prepared to take a firm initiative. The DOS and DOT were unlikely to act before someone else had moved first. No US carrier would take the initiative. The Europeans were divided and wanted to probe the American attitude rather than making bold suggestions. And Canada's envisaged role was that of a mediator rather than initiator.

In preparation for the US-Canada-ECAC tripartite meeting scheduled to be held in Washington in February 1981, the IATA Secretariat stepped up its efforts. Thus the Canadians were told — in highly optimistic terms — that 'high level contacts' in the DOS and DOT supported the 'new initiative' and that ECAC members were 'clearly positive.' In an intensive exchange of letters and personal meetings with ECAC representatives, IATA emphasized the promising signs on the American side. The 'emerging openmindedness' and 'increased understanding of multilateral coordination' on the part of American officials were noted, and much was made of the Boyd Hight speech. There were even expressions of cautious optimism about renewed CAB flexibility.

The tripartite meeting in Washington did not match the expectations of US flexibility. Yet the IATA Secretariat was not discouraged by this contemporary setback but redoubled its efforts and worked out more concrete proposals. It had become increasingly obvious that the other actors were looking to IATA for a compromise formula. Soon after the Washington talks, the IATA ExCom established a six-man North Atlantic task force, headed by the IATA President, to assist the DG in working out a detailed proposal.

The IATA task force produced a document in early April, outlining the basic parameters of a possible compromise formula. In soundings of individual member carriers operating North Atlantic routes, the proposal obtained general support, provided participation by the major US airlines and government support.

In effect, the IATA Secretariat did considerable behind-the-scenes work in connection with the 12 June US-ECAC meeting in Paris. Last-minute information from Washington indicated that the United States was looking for a smooth meeting to show the new administration's resolve and to avoid differences of view with the Europeans. The European side seemed somewhat more problematic. A DG report to the assembled ECAC Directors General of Civil Aviation a few days before the meeting met with passivity, and at the meeting there seemed to be fundamental disagreement on the approach to be taken. Yet the IATA Secretariat helped to arrange a prior meeting between ECAC and US officials, which seemed to have had a helpful effect in eliciting a positive American reaction to ECAC's main points of principle.

The meeting itself gave useful indications for future negotiations. The DOT had obviously taken the lead in formulating US aviation policy. At the meeting, only the DOT representative spoke on the US side, whereas the three CAB members present all kept silent.

A new US-ECAC meeting was scheduled for 27 July. Developments on the US side did not induce excessive optimism concerning a compromise. The DOT had encountered resistance from the CAB, Department of Justice and the Council of Economic Advisers in its efforts to remove the SCO and find a rapprochement with the European governments which would allow US carriers to participate in tariff coordination. The US draft position for the upcoming meeting was a 60 percent price zone subject to double disapproval (i.e., carriers would be allowed a 60 percent fare flexibility in relation to an agreed reference point, unless *both* civil aviation authorities involved disapproved the fare). The traditional US carriers, led by Pan Am and TWA, wished to retain the opportunity to join IATA tariff coordination if they wanted, but found the approach of IATA's working group 'too structured.' Newly established US airlines, on the other hand, wanted no return to a tariff coordination system which might jeopardize their ability to offer low fares to gain or maintain market shares.

The ECAC position, however, had crystallized to some extent. There was general acceptance of common principles but probably wide differences in details concerning the nature of a new tariff system. At the carrier level there appeared to be a fragile coalition around the principles suggested by the IATA task force, but again wide variance concerning details. In any event, the Europeans were not likely to trade the SCO for a 'double disapproval' agreement.

In this situation the IATA Secretariat saw as its mission to 'keep governments talking' so that the effectiveness of the SCO would be further postponed. And in the hope that the discussions would lead toward some 'middle ground,' IATA continued to promote its 'new initiative' thinking, particularly with US carriers.

Following the inconclusive 27–28 July US-ECAC meeting a chain of developments in the United States changed the bargaining premises. First, President Reagan asked the CAB to defer the SCO deadline. The Reagan intervention was prompted by his desire to avoid antagonizing nations that cooperated with the United States during the air-traffic disruptions resulting from the US air controllers' strike in May 1981. In his letter to CAB Chairman Marvin Cohen, President Reagan emphasized that it was 'essential that the U.S. take every reasonable step to reassure the international aviation community of our willingness to address matters of common concern in a cooperative manner' (quoted in Haanappel, 1983: 162).

Then, President Reagan appointed a new CAB Chairman, Dan McKinnon, who sought to balance consumer and carrier interests. 'If the public is going to be served,' McKinnon said in his first major speech, 'those who serve the public must make a profit' (CAB, 1982). Around the same time, a number of influential US airlines, bleeding red ink, announced their intention to return to tariff coordination. A final and key factor was that in the budget deliberations of the US Congress, a rider was attached to the Administrative Funding Bill, denying funds for the implementation of the Show Cause Order.

After both sides had consented to the principle of fare bands at the July US-ECAC meeting, the chief points at issue were, first, the degree of fare flexibility and, second, the participation of non-IATA carriers. The Americans advocated wide fare zones, the Europeans wanted narrow ones. And the Europeans, especially the British, demanded that non-IATA carriers be allowed to participate in — and be granted antitrust immunity for — fare coordination in North Atlantic Traffic Conferences.

At a new tripartite meeting in Paris on 16–18 December, a preliminary agreement was hammered out, the details of which were to be prepared before the new US-ECAC meeting in late February 1982. The Americans refused to give any guarantees concerning the participation of non-IATA carriers until the agreement had been signed. The British, for their part, threatened withdrawal from the proposed agreement unless non-member participation was allowed. In the end, however, this remaining difference did not forestall an accommodation.

On 26 February the US-ECAC meeting in Paris did indeed reach tentative agreement on a Memorandum of Understanding which granted antitrust immunity for North Atlantic tariff coordination but left details concerning pricing zones, reference fares and discount fares unresolved. In March the CAB postponed indefinitely the termination date of the SCO, and after the finalization of the Memorandum of Understanding in May, the CAB in September granted antitrust immunity for non-IATA carriers' participation in North Atlantic fare talks.

As part of the US domestic policy of deregulation, the CAB was abolished on 31 December 1984. Most of its functions were taken over by the Department of Transportation. The Show Cause Order died with the CAB.

## Conclusions

The US bilateral negotiation offensive and the Show Cause Order were obviously linked but not necessarily well orchestrated. It is significant that the 1978 policy document guiding subsequent bilateral negotiations made no mention of IATA fare setting at all (cf. Harbison, 1982: 210). And one of the participants in the SCO process, James Atwood (1980:

1071–2), who served as Deputy Assistant Secretary in the DOS with responsibility for aviation affairs in 1978–9, has noted retrospectively:

> The CAB did not act wisely by attacking IATA's antitrust immunity. The Board was on sound ground under both domestic and international law for opening its investigation, and it presumably did not predict the degree of reaction abroad. But the threat to apply U.S. antitrust to IATA simply hardened foreign opposition to U.S. policies, perhaps with the short-run consequence of jeopardizing additional liberal agreements.

Both the bilateral negotiations and the SCO process revealed divergent perceptions among the Americans and their counterparts. Now, as in 1944, the rest of the world tended to distrust the motives behind America's 'open skies' policy. 'Survival of the fittest' in international aviation inevitably entails 'survival of the fattest,' and there was widespread apprehension that the American preaching of *laissez-faire* really meant '*laissez-nous-faire*.' The desire to secure greater market shares by flooding international markets with a multitude of strong US airlines rather than unwavering faith in free competition was seen as the ultimate purpose of US policy, especially since the United States did not prove enthusiastic about deregulating other industries where it was competitively weaker, such as shipping. Hence the United States was again accused of 'aero-imperialism' by European and Third World representatives alike (cf., e.g., Stainton, 1979; Thomson, 1979; Cruz, 1979).

American perceptions were heavily influenced by the thinking of those academic economists who came to dominate the CAB in the late 1970s. Alfred Kahn, 'the high priest of deregulation,' was Professor of Economics at Cornell University, and his closest associate was another articulate academic, Mike Levine, 'a supercharged economics lecturer from Los Angeles' (Sampson, 1985: 170). They acted on the firm belief that greater competition and reliance on market forces nationally as well as internationally would yield substantial *consumer* benefits. Kahn argued in 1978 that the protectionists in the world were in a losing fight: 'It will become more and more difficult for them to hide behind protectionist walls, because there is a huge fifth column behind those walls — their own travellers and shippers' (quoted in Harbison, 1982: 52).

It was the unconventional traveller, in particular, who was assumed to reap benefits from the new US policy:

The United States believes strongly that air travel should not be the prerogative only of business travelers and the very rich. Given today's aviation technology, there is no question that a much greater range of service can be made available to those of us who are not in either of these exclusive categories. In the long run, competition is the simplest and most efficient way to insure the proper mix of service. (Cohen, 1980b.)

Since, according to this view, consumers in all countries would be the winners, there ought to be widespread support for US policy. Thus in 1978 the US member of the ICAO Air Transport Committee 'stated that he had expected that Committee Members would have expressed concern for the consumers, but he was surprised that even Members from the developing countries spoke only for the carriers' (ICAO, 1978b; 43).

Though not shared by all US policy-makers, the theoretical economic argument in favor of free competition squared well with considerations based on American self-interest. Hence, despite divergences in the respective camps, the Americans and their counterparts regarded the possible revision of the Chicago-Bermuda regime from different vantage points.

In their efforts to change the existing aviation regime, the Americans sought for more competition, less government intervention and less multilateralism. The outcome, as we have seen, was a compromise in which competitive elements were added to the existing multilateral framework. Ironically, a greater degree of government involvement was a significant by-product of the SCO process and the US-ECAC agreement. This possibility was, in fact, foreseen by some US policy-makers. DOS Deputy Assistant Secretary Boyd Hight, for example, observed in 1980 that 'one of the ironies of our liberal policy is that in some respects it may increase rather than diminish government's role' (quoted in Harbison, 1982: 208).

Networking was a prominent feature in the bargaining process triggered by the SCO. Taking the initiative in mobilizing the potential network, IATA assumed and maintained a linking-pin position. Above all, the IATA Secretariat played a key role in *information processing* within the network mobilized as a result of the SCO.

First, the IATA Secretariat was consistently in possession of solid intelligence. This applied, in particular, to the internal US scene. The Secretariat received inside information about what was going on in Washington through several different channels. At the outset of the SCO process, IATA hired a legal counsel in Washington who was a former Deputy Assistant Secretary of State for Economic and Business Affairs. In May 1979, a retired DOS official with long and distinguished service, most recently as Director of the Office of Aviation, joined the IATA Secretariat as the organization's representative and liaison officer in Washington. In addition, IATA could rely on other sources of information. All provided the Secretariat with reliable information from well-placed sources in all of the American agencies involved. This meant that the IATA Secretariat consistently knew of the US moves before they were made and could plan their own actions accordingly.

Second, IATA served as a kind of 'clearing-house' for SCO-related information. The Secretariat continuously solicited and obtained information from all relevant actors which it then disseminated, especially via member carriers and carrier organizations. Other actors frequently approached IATA for information, and IATA officials on several occasions acted as 'brokers' by passing on pertinent information from one actor to another. In short, a large portion of the information concerning the SCO which passed through the international aviation network was either initiated by, or mediated through, the IATA Secretariat.

In the earliest stage of the SCO proceedings the IATA Secretariat saw the creation of a strong coalition in support of multilateralism, and thereby of IATA, as a primary objective. Foreign governments and the US DOS were viewed as the pillars of such a coalition. This proved to be a correct assessment. 'Diplomatic considerations are primary reasons for our decision to extend immunity to the new IATA,' CAB

Chairman Marvin Cohen (1980a) told the ICAO Special Air Transport Conference in 1980. And all the officials interviewed on the American side share the impression that foreign policy considerations, rather than substantive arguments, were ultimately decisive in forcing the CAB to back down. One leading CAB official admits furthermore that the concerns of Third World airlines, in particular, influenced the CAB's partial retreat — the very airlines to which IATA assigned priority in its mobilization efforts.

No explicit issue linkage was attempted by the involved actors. Throughout the deliberations of a revised aviation regime there was diffuse issue linkage, insofar as foreign policy arguments loomed large: the absence of consensus between the Americans and the rest of the world on an international aviation regime would ultimately have a negative effect on America's interstate relations generally.

Gradually, the IATA Secretariat assumed the role of unofficial mediator and tried to find a middle ground between the Americans and the Europeans — governments as well as airlines — which would at the same time be beneficial for the organization itself. It took the initiative in outlining and promoting a compromise proposal which involved important organizational change for IATA. The 'new initiative' idea, though not inspired by the organization's constituents, the airlines, was developed within the framework of general directions and ultimately endorsed by the constituents.

As the preceding analysis has demonstrated, the ability of the IATA Secretariat to build cross-national coalitions and to assume a mediatory role with ultimate impact on intergovernmental negotiations was predicated on the existence of internal disagreements within the main state actor, the United States. Moreover, the pluralistic US political system, where lobbying by various interest groups is considered part of the game, provided an ideal setting for an active linking-pin organization.

The multitude of aviation nations and organizations underscored the need for some kind of 'broker.' With the advent of Third World nations after World War II, the international aviation community was virtually global in scope but also more diversified than ever. To establish consensus on a revised aviation regime either through a series of bilateral or in multilateral negotiations would have been extremely cumbersome, if at all possible. It is significant that the eventual compromise was worked out within the bilaterals US-ECAC framework.

In short, it is impossible to understand the US failure to change the Chicago-Bermuda regime without looking into the complex bargaining process initiated as a result of the new US policy — a process in which the mobilization of a transnational network played a key role.

This last paragraph tells it all — The 'regime' was not changed at all significantly & the earlier assertion that sovereignty was the central principle of the regime looses its force in this economic/ideological tale

# Conclusion

In the preceding chapters I have outlined different explanatory models and applied them to three episodes of regime creation, change and maintenance in international aviation. Rather than relying on any one model, I have probed the ability of several models to account for the observed regime dynamics. This approach is reminiscent of Graham Allison's (1971) noted study of the Cuban missile crisis, in which he made different 'cuts' at the same reality by using alternative analytical lenses. Allison demonstrated that any given conceptual frameworks serve as beacons that guide and sensitize the researcher to some sets of data and potential explanations as well as blinders, desensitizing him to evidence that might support competing explanations.

My discussion of alternative explanatory models has proceeded from higher to lower levels of generality and simplicity. I have thus followed the advice of Keohane and Nye (1977: 58) to 'seek explanation with simple models and add complexity as necessary.' Parsimony is a scientific virtue.  The purpose of theory is to simplify reality in order to make it more comprehensible.

Moving from a simpler explanatory level to a more complex one implies a loss in terms of parsimony, at the same time as the data requirements expand. Put differently, the information costs increase, as complexity is added. For instance, the information required by the process model outlined in this study dwarfs that needed by structural or situational models. There are thus practical as well as epistemological reasons for preferring a simpler model. If it yields satisfactory explanations there is no need to add complexity to a simplified model. If it does not, complexity may be added gradually by relaxing the simplifying assumptions of the original model step-by-step.

Following Keohane and Nye, I began with economic

models which ignore political aspects entirely and see regime change as a result of technological change and supply/demand dynamics. In view of the unsatisfactory explanatory power of these factors, the next logical step was to add politics in a relatively parsimonious way by turning to structural models — focussing on either overall or issue structure — and seeing whether these, alone or in conjunction with economic models, could explain regime change.

As this level proved insufficient in explaining all instances of regime dynamics in international aviation, situational factors were added. Situational models add complexity by allowing for individual choice by rational actors. According to this perspective, decisions by governments to create, maintain or change regimes are not determined solely by existing power structures but constitute conscious choices in dilemma-like situations.

Most attempts at explaining regime change stop at this level (cf., e.g., Keohane, 1984). However, the inability of the three explanatory modes — economic, structural and situational — to explain satisfactorily all the observed instances of regime change in international aviation, either individually or jointly, led me to probe a fourth model which focusses on the political process leading to international regime agreements and which relaxes the situational model's assumptions of rational and unitary state actors. This model regards regimes as outcomes of multilevel bargaining processes where the existence or absence of transnational networks is of special significance.

As demonstrated by Allison (1971), different models not only produce different answers to the same question; often they frame the question differently. Expressed more metaphorically:

Conceptual models not only fix the mesh of the nets that the analyst drags through the material in order to explain a particular action, they also direct him to cast his nets in select ponds, at certain depths, in order to catch the fish he is after. (Allison, 1971: 4.)

Thus, the questions posed in this study of regime evolution in international aviation — 'Why was the "unlimited sovereignty" regime created in 1919?'; 'Why was it changed in

1944?'; and 'Why did the attempted regime change in the late 1970s fail?' — are interpreted differently by the four models used in the study. The economic and structural models both look for 'because of' answers to these 'why's.' For the economic model the question is: What underlying technological or supply/demand factors relating to the air transport industry led to regime creation, change and maintenance? 'Why,' in the structural interpretation, translates into 'what shifts in the overall or issue-specific power structure elicited the three regime episodes?'

The answers of the situational model are more of the 'in order to' variety. Governments create international regimes in order to deal with the collective irrationality resulting from individual rationality. The puzzle for the situational model is: Which aspects of, or changes in, the choice situation facing the individual governments made them choose collective rather than individual action?

The process model, finally, offers 'as a result of' answers to the basic questions, tracing the political process leading up to the agreements to create, change, or maintain an international regime. The question 'why' is understood as 'from what kind of bargaining process did these agreements emerge?'

The fact that our four models not only give different answers but, to some extent, also ask different questions raises the question of whether they are incompatible or complementary. Indeed, there are certain apparent incompatibilities. For example, the structural model would predict that the United States, by virtue of its considerable issue-specific power, would be more successful in its attempt to change the Chicago-Bermuda regime; whereas the process model explains why the United States failed. On the other hand, some of the models display equally obvious similarities. Both the structural and the situational models see war as a catalyst of regime change, and the number of actors is an important variable in situational as well as process explanations.

My contention is that the models are complementary in the sense that neither model can provide a full explanation, but a combination of models is warranted. One model may apply quite well for one episode, but poorly for another. Having looked at the four models separately in previous chapters, let us now see what combinations of models explain each of the three observed episodes of regime dynamics.

The puzzle surrounding the creation of the first aviation regime in 1919 is: why did airspace sovereignty rather than air freedom become the guiding principle of the regime? After all, it could be argued that 'of the three elements — land, sea, and air — the last is the least national and nationalizable' (Goedhuis, 1942: 613). Yet the principle of national sovereignty became more salient in international aviation than in international shipping where the right of 'innocent passage' in territorial waters is granted by international law and traffic rights between ports do not have to be negotiated bilaterally between governments.

As has been pointed out several times in the preceding analysis, *timing* provides the chief key to this puzzle. The regime was drafted right after World War I, in which military aviation proved its worth for the first time. This points to structural and situational explanations which both regard war as a catalyst of regime creation and change. And a combination of structural and situational factors does indeed go a long way toward explaining the contents of the regime.

Both the overall structure and the issue structure emerging from the war were diffuse. The unanimous acceptance of the sovereignty principle reflected the absence of a hegemon in the international system generally and in international aviation in particular. Unrestricted sovereignty implied equality between states, large and small. In general, the concept of sovereignty stipulates the legal equality of all states. 'Equality,' says Hans Morgenthau (1966: 315), 'is nothing but a synonym for sovereignty.' By the same token, the sovereignty principle came to function as an equalizer in international aviation. By being able to open and close its airspace to others at will, every state could in principle avoid foreign penetration and domination.

Another aspect of the sovereignty principle, as applied to international air transport, was that it allocated the ultimate authority over aviation matters to *states*. Other actors, such as international organizations or airlines, were relegated to the background. This can be accounted for by the situational model. If before the war a future air regime had been discussed in terms of a trade-off between commercial and military interests, security concerns now took the upper hand. The payoff structure, in other words, had changed dramatically as a result of the war. As security considerations came to overshadow commercial ones, the necessity for strict state authority was underscored.

The process model adds marginally to structural and situational explanations. First, it reminds us that the decision-makers in 1919 did not see the situation facing them as an either/or choice, as the situational model portrays it. Nor can the outcome of the negotiations in Paris be characterized as a compromise. Rather, the 1919 regime reflected a broad consensus around the notion of airspace sovereignty. The perceptions of the decision-makers had changed as a result of the war. The perceptual shift was connected with a change of bargaining actors. The informal network of jurists, which had played the major role in regime deliberations before the war, was supplanted by an informal network of military officers. Finally, the situational and process models both direct attention to the fact that the relatively limited number of aviation nations in 1919 facilitated the attainment of an international agreement.

In sum, the combined explanation of the 1919 regime looks something like this: The perceived costs of a regime based on air freedom had risen dramatically as a result of World War I. As military considerations came to the fore, so did informal military networks. In the absence of any hegemon, a regime based on airspace sovereignty was then the natural outcome. This rendition omits economic explanatory factors. Certainly, World War I entailed significant technological developments, and a situation of 'surplus capacity' existed at the end of the war. But neither development had any direct effect on the 1919 regime. It was the *military* rather than the technological aspects of the development during the war that worried decision-makers; and the added supply of airplanes and pilots after the war was matched by increasing demand.

Similarly, neither technology nor surplus capacity can account for the regime change after World War II. Issue structuralism, on the other hand, provides a powerful explanation of the hybrid character of the Chicago-Bermuda regime. Britain's geographic leverage in combination with the state of the technology, which did not permit long-haul flights without intermediate refueling stops, explains why the United States, despite its overwhelming lead in air transport, was unable to establish a regime based on free competition.

The marginal contribution of the situational model consists of pointing to factors which made an agreement harder to reach than after World War I. The situation in 1944 was much more ambiguous. First, it cannot be represented as a clear-cut choice between two basic alternatives, as in 1919, but rather as interlocking 'sub-dilemmas.' Second, whereas air warfare had again demonstrated the need for airspace sovereignty, negative experiences of bilateral 'horse trading' under the 'unrestricted sovereignty' regime pointed to the need for more cooperative arrangements. Finally, the number of actors in international air transport had increased considerably.

These two themes — the bipolar issue structure and the difficulties inherent in the ambiguous situation after World War II — are amplified by the process model. The bargaining strategies of the United States and Britain were indeed to exploit their respective issue-specific power. And the eventual regime was in essence a US-British compromise. The ambiguity and complexity of the situation in the mid-1940s made international aviation a highly controversial issue both between and within nations. Divergent perceptions among the main actors led to mutual suspicions of ulterior motives. There was no informal network which could act as broker. As a result, an agreement could be reached only after a long and acrimonious bargaining process.

In short, the structural, situational and process models complement each other in accounting for the regime change after World War II. They all point in the same direction: there is little or no contradiction between the explanations offered by the models. Issue structuralism is obviously basic to an understanding of the Chicago-Bermuda regime; the situational and process explanations add details and complementary aspects.

Turning to the regime challenge in the late 1970s and its failure, our models appear more contradictory. The overriding question is: why did the United States not succeed in its effort to revise the Chicago-Bermuda regime? The structural model fails to provide a satisfactory explanation.

Although the regime challenge came at a time when there were cumulative signs of declining overall American power, there was no corresponding change of the issue-specific power structure in international air transport. The United States remained by far the strongest aviation nation and did not hesitate to exploit its issue-specific power. Therefore, according to the structural model, the United States should have been more successful in its efforts at regime change.

The situational model gives a hint of the obstacles to translating issue-specific power into regime change by pointing to the multitude of actors with different payoff structures than the United States. And the economic model offers an explanation of why the regime challenge came at the time it did: international air transport — especially on the North Atlantic routes — suffered from surplus capacity as a result of the introduction of wide-bodied jets, expanding charter operations and decreasing demand.

Yet only the process model can provide a satisfactory explanation of the end result of the US regime challenge. The main difference between the two previous regime episodes and the attempted regime change in the late 1970s was that a transnational, interorganizational network had been built up as a result of the Chicago-Bermuda regime. By challenging the regime, the United States also challenged and mobilized the network. This had several implications. First, the United States could not exploit its issue-specific power by applying 'divide-and-rule' methods bilaterally, but had to face a coalition of opponents. In mobilizing the network, its linking-pin organization, IATA, could exploit internal differences within the US aviation system. Moreover, by virtue of its linking-pin position, IATA was able to act as mediator in eventually reaching a compromise solution which amounted to changes within the existing regime rather than regime change.

The overall conclusions emerging from this summary of our three regime episodes are relativistic. Each model helps in explaining regime change or persistence for at least one of our three episodes, but no one model proves to be a panacea. The economic model is only marginally helpful. The structural model provides powerful explanations of the creation of the 1919 regime and, in particular, the regime change after World

War II; but it makes erroneous predictions concerning the recent regime challenge and fails to account for the American lack of success.

The situational model is somewhat problematic, at least in its most general formulation: it helps us understand why international regimes are created in general, but has little predictive value as to what kind of regime will be established in individual cases. In most international issue-areas there will almost always exist dilemma-like situations. One may therefore wonder whether the situational model is falsifiable, in the way that the structural model is. However, changes in payoff structures and players are elements of the situational model which are in principle falsifiable and which have some explanatory potency. In the case of international aviation, these aspects were particularly prominent in the creation of the first regime after World War I.

The process model, finally, added significant details to structural-situational explanations of the first two regime episodes. In the case of the attempted regime change in the late 1970s, it serves as an indispensable corrective to the structural model.

Is it not possible, then, to combine the four different models into an overall theory of regime change? I agree with Keohane and Nye's (1977: 59) conclusion concerning their explanatory models (which differ somewhat from the present ones): 'It would not be wise to develop a single amalgamated model; but under different conditions, different combinations of the models will provide the best explanations of international regime change and political outcomes.'

The structural and process models stand out as the most prominent and potent of the four models probed in this study. Structuralism constitutes the predominant mode of explanation in extant regime studies and has the advantage of parsimony. However, the most recent regime episode in international air transport reveals the danger of relying on structural explanations alone. The process model can serve as a valuable complement and corrective to structural explanations.

The less than successful US attempt to revise the existing regime in the late 1970s dramatizes the value of process

*[handwritten margin note at top: 'issue-areas' & 'regime' used interchangeably, or so it might seem. This allows different 'models' to be emphasized.]*

explanations. How representative, then, is this episode? What generalized conclusions can be drawn from it?

The nature of the bargaining processes and the existence or effectiveness of transnational networks obviously differ from issue-area to issue-area. It is a common contention that non-state actors are not allowed to play significant roles in issue-areas which touch upon 'high politics' and involve — directly or indirectly — state security. To some extent this is borne out by the regime development in international air transport. As long as security aspects were predominant, no transnational network emerged, and aviation issues were solved through interstate bargaining. Although national security considerations still enter international aviation policies, the issue-area has in recent times by and large remained outside the realm of 'high politics.' One may assume, then, that experiences in the aviation issue-area may be germane to other high-technology politico-economic issue-areas which, despite indirect links with military security, have not entered 'high politics.'

The virtual absence of East-West polarization is another significant characteristic of the aviation issue-area today, as the Soviet Union by and large stays outside the present international regime. The concentration of issue-specific power to relatively homogeneous and ideologically non-antagonistic industrialized countries probably facilitated IATA's efforts to act as broker and mediator and to use the aviation network to influence other actors in the late 1970s. In issue-areas with polar or hegemonic structures transnational networks will most likely be less influential in changing or maintaining international regimes.

*[handwritten margin note: This is central. The SU are part of a regime but not part of the 'formal' negotiations of it.]*

A related point concerns the setting in which regime discussions evolve. From the viewpoint of transnational networks and prospective linking-pin organizations, it obviously makes a difference whether the bargaining process involves — and is carried out in — pluralistic, open or authoritarian, closed societies. The pluralistic American aviation system with manifest disagreements between different agencies, where lobbying by various interest groups is considered part of the game, provided an ideal setting for an active linking-pin organization like IATA. As the Show Cause Order process demonstrated, the ability of an international organization's boundary-role occupants to reach into, and bring pressure to bear within, a given country depends on access to — and intelligence concerning — influential domestic groups; in other words, it implies a pluralist polity. In Robert Cox's (1969: 230) words, 'the prospects of system change through the agency of international organizations and their executive heads would seem to be linked to the progress of pluralism in polities.'

Furthermore, the existing Chicago-Bermuda aviation regime contributed to IATA's ability to assume a linking-pin position within the international aviation network by assigning important functions to the organization. As pointed out by several analysts, regimes may assume a life of their own and become important intervening variables. 'Once a regime is actually in place, it may develop a dynamics of its own that can alter not only related behavior and outcomes but also basic causal variables' (Krasner, 1982b: 500). To generalize, an explicit regime, based on written legal documents, which designates a specific organization as the central decision-making forum or even the regime caretaker, and which is adhered to by a large majority of states, appears to maximize the potential for that particular organization to effectively assume a linking-pin position. Issue-areas characterized by non-regime situations or regimes based on tacit understandings, without a broad following, seem to provide a more uncertain, riskier environment for an organization aspiring to a linking-pin position, but may also offer opportunities for enterprising boundary-role occupants. The worst kind of regime, from the viewpoint of a prospective linking-pin organization, is probably an explicit and widely adhered-to regime which does not bestow any significant role upon that organization.

Having looked at the characteristics of issue-areas where the lessons of international aviation may be applicable, let me finally turn to a discussion of generalizable organization characteristics based on the IATA experience. Which background factors account for the ability of (the boundary-role occupants of) a given organization to assume and maintain a linking-pin position and use a transnational network to influence other actors in regime deliberations? My tentative listing of relevant background factors includes five variable clusters under the rubrics of reachability, mobility, conspicuousness, constituents and leadership.

*Reachability*. In order to assume an effective linking-pin position, an organization needs to have a location in the issue-specific network which allows it to reach, and to be reached by, other important organizational actors. Multiplexity of direct and indirect links with these actors can be expected to enhance the leverage of the prospective linking-pin organization (Aldrich, 1979: 336).

As we have seen, IATA had such a location in the international aviation network that it could indeed reach, and be reached by, the main organizational actors. The multiplex indirect and direct links with national governments and agencies were particularly significant. Via other organizations, IATA could even reach remote governments whose flag carriers were not members of IATA.

*Mobility*. Distance in terms of costs of transportation and communication is normally considered an environmental restraint on organizational action (see, e.g., Thompson, 1967: 68). The extent to which an organization is able to overcome this restraint and to 'be present' at the deliberations of other actors either through personal travel or communications media is of obvious significance for its ability to assume a linking-pin position.

The IATA Secretariat displayed exceptional mobility in the SCO case. For IATA distance represents less of a restraint than for most other organizational actors. By having unrestrained access to air travel on member carriers and being hooked up to the airline-owned telex communication system (SITA), the IATA Secretariat is assured instant mobility and communication. Boundary-role personnel do indeed travel frequently — some in excess of a hundred days per year. To be sure, one interviewed IATA official suggested that John Kenneth Galbraith's comment aimed at John Foster Dulles — 'travelling is a substitute for thinking' — may apply to the 'fire-brigade' behavior of the IATA Secretariat as well. Yet the on-the-spot presence of IATA personnel wherever a relevant issue is dealt with is considered by most respondents to be an important and frequently necessary asset. And the presence of IATA personnel at important SCO deliberations of other actors in combination with frequent informal, face-to-face encounters with key actors was a key element in IATA's successful mobilization of the aviation network in the late 1970s.

*Conspicuousness.* The broker role of a linking-pin organization is presumably facilitated by a relatively low profile. A high-profile organization, which attracts a lot of public interest and media coverage and is matter for controversy, seems less equipped for a linking-pin position.

IATA's public image is that of a 'whipping boy.' In the words of one respondent, 'IATA has become a four-letter word.' Its constituents, the airlines, have in fact contributed to this image by using IATA as a convenient scapegoat to blame for unpopular fares and regulations *vis-à-vis* customers. This unfavorable public image necessitates a low IATA profile in political and diplomatic interactions. This is well understood by the Secretariat and is also in the interest of the airlines. 'Quiet diplomacy' is therefore the key word used by boundary-role occupants of the IATA Secretariat to describe their activity. There is a strong realization that their diplomatic efforts can be successful only as long as they are not well known or advertised.

Throughout the SCO proceedings, the importance of maintaining a low profile was emphasized in intra-Secretariat strategy discussions. Whereas IATA effectively publicized its public position, its behind-the-scenes influence and mediation attempts did not attract media attention.

*Constituents.* The balance of capabilities — especially expertise — between the boundary-role occupants of an organization and its constituents is another factor of importance. Robert McLaren (1980: 135–6), in his study of specialized United Nations agencies, concluded that since the constituents of these organizations — governments and specialized government agencies — share the technical expertise and maintain a monopoly of political expertise, they will normally not allow the international secretariat to play a political role.

The balance of capabilities between the IATA Secretariat and its constituents diverges from the common pattern of shared technical expertise and constituent monopoly of political expertise. The IATA Secretariat, by contrast, has a high level of political expertise and the advantage of an overall

industry and international perspective, while sharing technical expertise with its constituents, the airlines. This leaves the
IATA Secretariat room for political maneuver. With respect
to the SCO issue, this meant that the IATA Secretariat's
detailed political actions were developed within the
framework of general instructions and endorsed *ex post facto*
by the constituents.

*Leadership.* Strong leadership is often considered a key to
the leverage of an international secretariat (see Cox, 1969). In
addition, for a prospective linking-pin organization it appears
important that boundary-role personnel occupy the most
central rather than peripheral positions within that organization.

The IATA Secretariat had a firm political leadership in the
Director General, Knut Hammarskjöld, and the Office of the
Director General. This applied to intra-Secretariat,
Secretariat-constituent as well as external relations. The
Director General was constantly engaging in personal
diplomacy at various levels around the globe. In other words,
he was the leading boundary-role occupant. Put differently,
boundary-role personnel occupied the most central rather
than peripheral positions in the IATA Secretariat — a
significant factor in accounting for IATA's linking-pin position.

To summarize, I have raised the question as to what
generalizable lessons concerning issue-areas and organizations can be learned from the regime evolution in international aviation. The final answer to this question, of course,
has to await further comparable case studies of other international issue-areas. Some steps have already been taken in
that direction. Tentative findings from the atomic energy,
refugees and maritime issue-areas tend to confirm the importance of the hypothesized issue-specific and organization-
specific factors in accounting for variance in network structure and performance (cf. Jönsson & Bolin, 1985; Jönsson,
1986b; McLaren, 1986).

Nor does this study provide a definite answer to the wider
question of the relative usefulness of different explanations
of regime creation, perseverance and change. Thus, my claim
for the process model is not that it should replace other
models but rather that regime analysis should be more

discriminating. I conclude by concurring with two of the pioneers in the study of international regimes who argued a decade ago that political scientists, like dentists, need both a variety of tools and the discrimination to know which to use at the right time (Keohane & Nye, 1977: 162). While the contribution of this study has primarily been in adding to the multitude of tools, we are still a long way from understanding fully the conditions under which the different tools are most helpful.

# Notes

## Chapter 2

1. Under the agreement, airlines are free to set their basic economy fares within 20 percent above or below a 'reference' fare level without government approval. The zone of flexibility for business-class fares is generally between 20 and 50 percent above the reference fare, whereas discount fares are allowed to drop 40–50 percent below the reference fare.

## Chapter 7

1. This section draws on interviews with IATA officials in May 1982 and with ICAO officials in April 1984.

2. Besides the interviews cited in note 1, the subsequent analysis draws on interviews conducted in April 1984 with representatives of US carriers and with American officials who served in the DOS, DOT and CAB at the time of the SCO proceedings. In addition, this analysis is based on internal IATA material to which I have been given generous access. The material consists of memos, letters, telexes, position papers and the like. Unless otherwise referenced, all quotations in this section are taken from this body of material.

# References

ALDRICH, H. (1979) *Organizations and Environments*, Englewood Cliffs: Prentice-Hall.

ALDRICH, H. (1982) 'The Origins and Persistence of Social Networks: A Comment,' in P.V. Marsden & N. Lin (eds) *Social Structure and Network Analysis*, Beverly Hills/London: Sage.

ALDRICH, H. & D.A. WHETTEN (1981) 'Organization-Sets, Action-Sets, and Networks: Making the Most of Simplicity,' in P.C. Nystrom & W.H. Starbuck (eds) *Handbook of Organizational Design*, vol. 1, New York: Oxford University Press.

ALLISON, G.T. (1971) *Essence of Decision: Explaining the Cuban Missile Crisis*, Boston: Little, Brown.

ATWOOD, J.R. (1980) 'International Aviation: How Much Competition, and How?' *Stanford Law Review* **32**: 1061–74.

AXELROD, R. (1984) *The Evolution of Cooperation*, New York: Basic Books.

AXELROD, R. & R.O. KEOHANE (1985) 'Achieving Cooperation under Anarchy: Strategies and Institutions,' *World Politics* **38**: 226–54.

BACHARACH, S.B. & E.J. LAWLER (1980) *Power and Politics in Organizations*, San Francisco: Jossey-Bass.

BECKER, B. (1967) *Dreams and Realities of the Conquest of the Skies*, New York: Atheneum.

BERGESEN, H.O. (1984) 'Norms Count, But Power Decides: International Regimes — Wishful Thinking or Realities?' paper prepared for ISA (International Studies Association) convention, Atlanta, 27–31 March.

BERLE, A.A., Jr. (1945) 'Freedom of the Air,' in *Blueprint for World Civilization: The Chicago International Conference of 1944 as Viewed by Four Members of the United States Delegation in Recent Magazine Articles*, Washington, D.C.: Department of State Publication 2348.

BERLE, A.A., Jr. (1973) *Navigating the Rapids 1918–1971: From the Papers of Adolf A. Berle*, New York: Harcourt Brace Jovanovich.

BISHOP, W.A. (1944) *Winged Peace*, New York: The Viking Press.

BRANCKER, J.W.S. (1977) *IATA and What It Does*, Leyden: Sijthoff.

BROOKS, P.W. (1961) *The Modern Airliner*, London: Putnam.

BROOKS, P.W. (1961) *The Modern Airliner*, London: Putnam.

BURDEN, W.A.M. (1945) 'Opening the Sky: American Proposals at Chicago,' in *Blueprint for World Civilization: The Chicago International Conference of 1944 as Viewed by Four Members of the United States Delegation in Recent Magazine Articles*, Washington, D.C.: Department of State Publication 2348.

BURTON, J.W. (1972) *World Society*, London: Cambridge University Press.

*BUSINESS WEEK* (1981) 'Is the U.S. Sabotaging Its International Airlines?' 26 January: 36–41.

CAB (1978) 'Agreements Adopted by the International Air Transport Association Relating to the Traffic Conferences: Order to Show Cause,' Washington, D.C.: US CAB Order 78–6–78.

CAB (1980) 'Agreement Adopted by the International Air Transport Association Relating to the Traffic Conferences: Order and Statement of Tentative Conclusions,' Washington, D.C.: US CAB Order 80–4–113.

CAB (1982) 'CAB Chairman McKinnon Calls for Pragmatic International Aviation Policy, Cites Renewed Resolve to Assure U.S. Carriers Fair Deal,' *CAB News*, 16 February.

CHUANG, R.Y. (1972) *The International Air Transport Association: A Case Study of Quasi-Governmental Organization*, Leyden: Sijthoff.

CLAUDE, I.L. (1964) *Swords into Plowshares: The Problems and Progress of International Organization*, New York: Random House.

COHEN, M.S. (1979) 'Six Myths About U.S. International Air Transportation Policy,' paper presented at ITA (Institut du transport aérien) Think Tank on International Air Transportation, Paris, 8 June.

COHEN, M.S. (1980a) 'A Presentation to SATC concerning the CAB's Proposed IATA Decision,' ICAO Second Air Transport Conference, 12 February.

COHEN, M.S. (1980b) 'Can Airline Deregulation Work in International Air Transportation?' lecture at MIT summer course 'Air Transportation: Management, Economics, and Planning,' 25 June.

COLEGROVE, K.W. (1930) *International Control of Aviation*, Boston: World Peace Foundation.

CONFÉRENCE INTERNATIONALE (1910) *Conférence internationale de navigation aérienne: Procès-verbaux des séances, Paris, 18 mai–29 juin 1910*, Paris: Imprimerie nationale.

COOK, D. (1945) *The Chicago Aviation Agreements: An Approach to World Policy*, New York: American Enterprise Association.

COOPER, J.C. (1947) *The Right to Fly*, New York: Henry Holt & Co.

COOPER, J.C. (1968) *Explorations in Aerospace Law*, Montreal: McGill University Press.

CORBETT, D. (1965) *Politics and the Airlines*, London: George Allen & Unwin.

COWHEY, P.F. & E. LONG (1983) 'Testing Theories of Regime Change: Hegemonic Decline or Surplus Capacity?' *International Organization* **37**: 157–83.

COX, R.W. (1969) 'The Executive Head: An Essay on Leadership in International Organization,' *International Organization* **23**: 205–30.

COX, R.W. & H.K. JACOBSON (1973) *The Anatomy of Influence: Decision Making in International Organization*, New Haven: Yale University Press.

CRAWFORD, B. & S. LENWAY (1985) 'Decision Modes and International Regime Change: Western Collaboration and East-West Trade,' *World Politics* **37**: 375–402.

CRUZ, R.A. Jr. (1979) 'American Aero-Imperialism: Issues and Alternatives,' address to International Aviation Club, Washington, D.C., 19 June.

DARGAN, M. (1976) 'The North Atlantic,' Geneva: IATA.

DAVIES, R.E.G. (1964) *A History of the World's Airlines*, London: Oxford University Press.

DRUCKMAN, D. (1978) 'Boundary Role Conflict: Negotiation as Dual Responsiveness,' in I.W. Zartman (ed.) *The Negotiation Process: Theories and Applications*, Beverly Hills: Sage.

EMME, E.M. (ed.) (1959) *The Impact of Air Power*, Princeton, N.J.: Van Nostrand.

FALK, R.A. (1977) 'Contending Approaches to World Order,' *Journal of International Affairs* **31**: 171–98.

FISHER, R. & W. URY (1983) *Getting to Yes: Negotiating Agreement Without Giving In*, New York: Penguin.

GIBBS-SMITH, C.H. (1967) *A Brief History of Flying: From Myth to Space Travel*, London: Her Majesty's Stationery Office.

GILPIN, R. (1975) *U.S. Power and the Multinational Corporation*, New York: Basic Books.

GILPIN, R. (1981) *War and Change in World Politics*, Cambridge: Cambridge University Press.

GOEDHUIS, D. (1942) 'Civil Aviation after the War,' *American Journal of International Law* **36**: 596–613.

GORDENKER, L. & P.R. SAUNDERS (1978) 'Organisation Theory and International Organisation,' in P. Taylor & A.J.R. Groom (eds) *International Organisation: A Conceptual Approach*, London: Frances Pinter.

HAANAPPEL, P.P.C. (1983) *Pricing and Capacity Determination in International Air Transport*, Deventer: Kluwer.

HAAS, E.B. (1964) *Beyond the Nation-State*. Stanford: Stanford University Press.

HAAS, E.B. (1980) 'Why Collaborate? Issue-Linkage and International Regimes,' *World Politics* 32: 357–405.

HAAS, E.B. (1982) 'Words Can Hurt You; or, Who Said What to Whom about Regimes,' *International Organization* 36: 207–43.

HALL, M. & W. PECK (1941) 'Wings for the Trojan Horse,' *Foreign Affairs* 19: 347–69.

HAMMARSKJÖLD, K. (1976) 'The New Economic Environment and Its Effects on Air Transport,' address to International World Airports Conference, Brighton, 5 May.

HAMMARSKJÖLD, K. (1977) 'Air Cargo Prospects,' address to Freight Seminar, Gothenburg, 17 March.

HAMMARSKJÖLD, K. (1978a) 'International Air Transport, Tariffs and Trade,' address to the Royal Institute of International Affairs, London, 25 April.

HAMMARSKJÖLD, K. (1978b) 'Address to the International Chamber of Commerce,' Orlando, Florida, 4 October.

HAMMARSKJÖLD, K. (1979) 'Dynamic Developments in Air Transport and Dramatic Changes in IATA,' address to Royal Aeronautic Society, London, 26 April.

HARBISON, P. (1982) 'Liberal Bilateral Agreements of the United States: A Dramatic New Pricing Policy,' Montreal: LL.M. Thesis, McGill University.

HERNES, G. (ed.) (1978) *Forhandlingsøkonomi og blandningsadministrasjon*, Oslo: Universitetsforlaget.

HERZ, J.H. (1959) *International Politics in the Atomic Age*, New York: Columbia University Press.

HIGHT, B.B. (1980) 'Deregulation Abroad: A Game without Rules,' speech to the International Aviation Club, Washington, D.C., 18 November.

HILDRETH, C.H. & B.C. NALTY (1969) *1001 Questions Answered About Aviation History*, New York: Dodd, Mead & Company.

HJERN, B. & D.O. POTTER (1981) 'Implementation Structures: A New Unit of Administrative Analysis,' *Organization Studies* 2/3: 211–27.

HOAGLAND, J.H. (1978) 'The U.S. and European Aerospace Industries and Military Exports to the Less Developed Countries,' in U. Ra'anan, R.L. Pfaltzgraff, Jr. & G. Kemp (eds) *Arms Transfers to the Third World: The Military Buildup in Less Industrial Countries*, Boulder, Co.: Westview.

HOFSTADTER, D.R. (1983) 'Metamagical Themas: Computer Tournaments of the Prisoner's Dilemma Suggest How Cooperation Evolves,' *Scientific American* **248**: 16–26.

HUTCHISON, K. (1944) *Freedom of the Air*, New York: Public Affairs Committee.

IATA (1978) *World Air Transport Statistics, 1977*, Geneva: IATA.

IATA (1980) 'The International Multilateral Interline System: Its Benefits and Requirements,' Geneva: IATA.

ICAO (1971) *ICAO Assembly, Eighteenth session, Vienna, 15 June–7 July 1971: Minutes of the plenary meetings*, ICAO Doc. 8963, A18 Min. P/1–16.

ICAO (1977) *ICAO Special Air Transport Conference, Montreal, 13–26 April 1977: Report*, ICAO Doc. 9199, SATC.

ICAO (1978a) *ICAO Council, 95th session: Minutes of 16th meeting, 15 December 1978*, ICAO Doc. 9524-C/1047, C-Min. 95/16.

ICAO (1978b) *ICAO Air Transport Committee, 95th session of the Council: Minutes of the 12th meeting, 12 December 1978*, AT Min. 95–12.

ICAO (1980) *ICAO Second Air Transport Conference, Montreal, 12–28 February 1980: Report*, ICAO Doc. 9297, AT Conf/2.

JACOBSON, H.K. (1979) *Networks of Interdependence*, New York: Alfred A. Knopf.

JERVIS, R. (1976) *Perception and Misperception in International Politics*, Princeton, N.J.: Princeton University Press.

JERVIS, R. (1978) 'Cooperation under the Security Dilemma,' *World Politics* **30**: 167–214.

JOHNSON, B. (1972) *Suveräniteten i havet och luftrummet*, Stockholm: Nordstedts.

JOHNSON, D.W. (1974) 'Communication and the Inducement of Cooperative Behavior in Conflicts: A Critical Review,' *Speech Monographs* **41**: 64–78.

JÖNSSON, C. (1981) 'Sphere of Flying: The Politics of International Aviation,' *International Organization* **35**: 273–302.

JÖNSSON, C. (1983) 'A Cognitive Approach to International Negotiation,' *European Journal of Political Research* **11**: 139–50.

JÖNSSON, C. (1986a) 'Interorganization Theory and International Organization,' *International Studies Quarterly* **30**: 39–57.

JÖNSSON, C. (1986b) 'Do Transnational Networks Matter?' paper prepared for ISA (International Studies Association) convention, Anaheim, Ca., 25–29 March.

JÖNSSON, C. & S. BOLIN (1985) 'IAEA's Role in the International Politics of Atomic Energy,' paper prepared for ISA (International Studies Association) convention, Washington, D.C., 5–9 March.

JUDGE, A.J.N. (1978) 'International Organisation Networks: A Complementary Perspective,' in P. Taylor & A.J.R. Groom (eds) *International Organisation: A Conceptual Approach*, London: Frances Pinter.

KAHN, A. (1978) 'Should We Be Searching for an International Order; or, How Chaotic is "Chaos"?' speech to the International Aviation Club, Washington, D.C., 16 May.

KALDOR, M. (1979) 'Economic Aspects of Arms Supply Policies in the Middle East,' in M. Leitenberg & G. Sheffer (eds) *Great Power Intervention in the Middle East*, New York: Pergamon.

KEOHANE, R.O. (1980) 'The Theory of Hegemonic Stability and Changes in International Economic Regimes, 1967–1977,' in O.R. Holsti, R.M. Siverson, & A.L. George (eds) *Change in the International System*, Boulder, Co.: Westview.

KEOHANE, R.O. (1982) 'The Demand for International Regimes,' *International Organization* 36: 325–55.

KEOHANE, R.O. (1984) *After Hegemony: Cooperation and Discord in the World Political Economy*, Princeton, N.J.: Princeton University Press.

KEOHANE, R.O. (1986) 'Reciprocity in International Relations,' *International Organization* 40: 1–27.

KEOHANE, R.O. & J.S. NYE (1975) 'International Interdependence and Integration,' in F.I. Greenstein and N.W. Polsby (eds) *Handbook of Political Science*, vol. 8, Reading, Mass.: Addison-Wesley.

KEOHANE, R.O. & J.S. NYE (1977) *Power and Interdependence*, Boston: Little, Brown.

KIHL, Y.W. (1971) *Conflict Issues and International Civil Aviation Decisions: Three Cases*, Denver, Co.: Monograph Series in World Affairs, University of Denver.

KILMARX, R.A. (1962) *A History of Soviet Air Power*, London: Faber & Faber.

KINDLEBERGER, C.P. (1981) 'Dominance and Leadership in the International Economy,' *International Studies Quarterly* 25: 242–54.

KRASNER, S.D. (1982a) 'Structural Causes and Regime Consequences: Regimes as Intervening Variables,' *International Organization* 36: 185–205.

KRASNER, S.D. (1982b) 'Regimes and the Limits of Realism: Regimes as Autonomous Variables,' *International Organization* 36: 497–510.

KUHN, A.K. (1910) 'The Beginnings of an Aerial Law,' *American Journal of International Law* 4: 109–32.

KUHN, AK (1920) "International Aerial Navigation and the Peace Conference,' *American Journal of International Law* **14**: 369-81.

LABOUR PARTY (1944) *Wings for Peace: Labour's Post-War Policy*, London: Labour Publications.

LAMPERT, D.E., L.C. FALKOWSKI, & R.W. MANSBACH (1978) 'Is There an International System?' *International Studies Quarterly* **22**: 143–66.

LEGREZ, F. (1982) 'Airline Subsidies,' in A. Kean (ed.) *Essays in Air Law*, The Hague: Martinus Nijhoff.

LEVINE, M.E. (1979) 'Requested Comments on Negotiation Strategies for Northern and Southern Europe,' CAB memorandum, 26 February.

LIPMAN, G.H. (1976) 'An Analysis of the North Atlantic 1964–1974: Regulatory/Governmental Considerations,' Geneva: IATA.

LIPSON, C. (1982) 'The Transformation of Trade: The Sources and Effects of Regime Change,' *International Organization* **36**: 417–55.

LISSITZYN, O.J. (1942) *International Air Transport and National Policy*, New York: Council on Foreign Relations.

LOWENFELD, A.F. (1975) 'A New Takeoff for International Air Transport,' *Foreign Affairs* **54**: 36–50.

LYCKLAMA à NIJEHOLT, J.F. (1910) *Air Sovereignty*, The Hague: Martinus Nijhoff.

McFARLAND, M.W. (1959) 'When the Airplane Was a Military Secret,' in E.M. Emme (ed.) *The Impact of Air Power*, Princeton, N.J.: Van Nostrand.

McLAREN, R.I. (1980) *Civil Servants and Public Policy: A Comparative Study of International Secretariats*, Waterloo, Ontario: Wilfrid Laurier Press.

McLAREN, R.I. (1986) 'Organizing the Safety of the Seas: An Investigation of Three Rationales for the Success of an IGO,' paper prepared for ISA (International Studies Association) convention, Anaheim, Ca., 25–29 March.

MACHIAVELLI, N. (1950) *The Prince and The Discourses*, New York: The Modern Library.

MAGDALÉNAT, J.-L. (1980) 'The Story of the Life and Death of the CAB Show Cause Order,' *Air Law* **5**: 83–98.

MANCE, O. (1943) *International Air Transport*, London: Oxford University Press.

MARCH, J.G. (ed.) (1965) *Handbook of Organizations*, Chicago: Rand McNally.

MATHU, E.W. (1979) 'Implications of Greater or Lesser Competition in International Civil Aviation on the Economic Development of LDCs,' paper presented at U.S. Department of State Symposium on International Aviation Policy, Kingston, Jamaica, 30 January–2 February.

MENDLOVITZ, S.H. (ed.) (1975) *On the Creation of a Just World Order: Preferred Worlds for the 1990s*, New York: The Free Press.

METCALFE, L. (1981) 'Designing Precarious Partnerships,' in P.C. Nystrom & W.H. Starbuck (eds) *Handbook of Organizational Design*, vol 1, New York: Oxford University Press.

MIDGAARD, K. & A. UNDERDAL (1977): 'Multiparty Conferences,' in D. Druckman (ed.) *Negotiations: Social-Psychological Perspectives*, Beverly Hills/London: Sage.

MORGAN, S.W. (1945) 'International Civil Aviation Conference at Chicago: What It Means to the Americas,' in *Blueprint for World Civilization: The Chicago International Conference of 1944 as Viewed by Four Members of the United States Delegation in Recent Magazine Articles*, Washington, D.C.: Department of State Publication 2348.

MORGENTHAU, H.J. (1966) *Politics among Nations: The Struggle for Power and Peace*, 3rd edn, New York: Alfred A. Knopf.

MORSE, E.L. (1976) *Modernization and the Transformation of International Relations*, New York: The Free Press.

NEALE, M.A. & M.H. BAZERMAN (1985) 'Perspectives for Understanding Negotiation: Viewing Negotiation as a Judgmental Process,' *Journal of Conflict Resolution* **29**: 33–55.

NYE, J.S. & R.O. KEOHANE (1971a) 'Transnational Relations and World Politics: An Introduction,' in R.O. Keohane & J.S. Nye (eds) *Transnational Relations and World Politics*, Cambridge, Mass.: Harvard University Press.

NYE, J.S. & R.O. KEOHANE (1971b) 'Transnational Relations and World Politics: A Conclusion,' in R.O. Keohane & J.S. Nye (eds) *Transnational Relations and World Politics*, Cambridge, Mass.: Harvard University Press.

NYSTROM, P.C. & W.H. STARBUCK (eds) (1981) *Handbook of Organizational Design*, 2 vols, New York: Oxford University Press.

ORGAN, D.W. (1971) 'Linking Pins Between Organizations and Environment,' *Business Horizons* **14**: 73–80.

OYE, K.A. (1985) 'Explaining Cooperation under Anarchy: Hypotheses and Strategies,' *World Politics* **38**: 1–24.

PILLAR, P.R. (1983) *Negotiating Peace: War Termination as a Bargaining Process*, Princeton, N.J.: Princeton University Press.

PRUITT, D.G. (1983) 'Strategic Choice in Negotiation,' *American Behavioral Scientist* **27**: 167–94.

PUCHALA, D.J. & R.F. HOPKINS (1982) 'International Regimes: Lessons from Inductive Analysis,' *International Organization* **36**: 245–75.

REIN, B.W. & B.L. McDONALD (1982) 'The "Legislative Hearing" on IATA Traffic Conferences — Creative Procedure in a High Stakes Setting,' in A. Kean (ed.) *Essays in Air Law*, The Hague: Martinus Nijhoff.

REYNOLDS, P.A. & R.D. McKINLAY (1979) 'The Concept of Interdependence: Its Uses and Misuses,' in K. Goldmann & G. Sjöstedt (eds) *Power, Capabilities, Interdependence*, Beverly Hills/London: Sage.

RICHARDS, H.E. (1912) *Sovereignty over the Air*, Oxford: Clarendon Press.

ROOS, L.L. & F.A. STARKE (1981) 'Organizational Roles,' in P.C. Nystrom & W.H. Starbuck (eds) *Handbook of Organizational Design* vol. 1, New York: Oxford University Press.

RUBIN, J.Z. (1983) 'Negotiation: An Introduction to Some Issues and Themes,' *American Behavioral Scientist* **27**: 135–47.

SAMPSON, A. (1985) *Empires of the Sky: The Politics, Contests and Cartels of World Airlines*, London: Coronet Books.

SCHELLING, T.C. (1963) *The Strategy of Conflict*, New York: Oxford University Press.

SCOTT, A.M. (1981) 'Organization Theory and IGOs,' paper prepared for ISA (International Studies Association) convention, Philadelphia, 18–21 March.

SEAWELL, W.T. (1981) 'Letter to CAB Chairman Marvin S. Cohen,' New York, 24 February.

SHARKANSKY, I. (1981) 'Intergovernmental Relations,' in P.C. Nystrom & W.H. Starbuck (eds) *Handbook of Organizational Design*, vol. 1. New York: Oxford University Press.

SMITH, H.I. (1950) *Airways Abroad: The Story of American World Air Routes*, Madison: University of Wisconsin Press.

SPERO, J.E. (1977) *The Politics of International Economic Relations*, London: George Allen & Unwin.

STAINTON, R. (1979) 'Deregulation: Quo Vadis? Where Indeed!' speech at International Aviation Conference, New York, 25 May.

STEIN, A.A. (1982) 'Coordination and Collaboration: Regimes in an Anarchic World,' *International Organization* **36**: 299–324.

STEINBRUNER, J.D. (1974) *The Cybernetic Theory of Decision*, Princeton: Princeton University Press.

STENELO, L.-G. (1972) *Mediation in International Negotiations*, Lund: Studentlitteratur.

STENELO,L.-G. (1984) *The International Critic*, Lund: Studentliteratur.

STRANGE, S. (1982) 'Cave! Hic Dragones: A Critique of Regime Analysis,' *International Organization* **36**: 479–96.

THAYER, F.C. (1965) *Air Transport Policy and National Security*, Chapel Hill: University of North Carolina Press.

THAYER, F.C. (1981) 'Organization Theory, Political Theory, and the International Arena: Some Hope But Very Little Time,' paper prepared for ISA (International Studies Association) convention, Philadelphia, 18–21 March.

THOMKA-GAZDIK, J.G. (1982) 'The Right to Fly — Review at Random,' in A. Kean (ed.) *Essays in Air Law*, The Hague: Martinus Nijhoff.

THOMPSON, J.D. (1967) *Organizations in Action*, New York: McGraw-Hill.

THOMSON, A. (1979) 'Experience on Transatlantic Routes with Competitive Fares and Liberal Charter Rules,' paper presented at US Department of State Symposium on International Aviation Policy, Kingston, Jamaica, 30 January–2 February.

THORNTON, R.L. (1970) *International Airlines and Politics*, Ann Arbor, Mich.: Michigan International Business Studies no. 13.

THORNTON, R.L. (1971) 'Governments and Airlines,' in R.O. Keohane & J.S. Nye (eds) *Transnational Relations and World Politics*, Cambridge, Mass.: Harvard University Press.

TICHY, N.M. (1981) 'Networks in Organizations,' in P.C. Nystrom & W.H. Starbuck (eds) *Handbook of Organizational Design*, vol. 2, New York: Oxford University Press.

TOMBS, L.C. (1936) *International Organization in European Air Transport*, New York: Columbia University Press.

UK SECRETARY OF STATE FOR AIR (1944) *International Air Transport*, London: His Majesty's Stationery Office, Cmd. 6561.

UN (1945) *Towards Freedom in the Air: The Story of the International Civil Aviation Conference, November 1st–December 7th, 1944*, New York: United Nations Information Office.

US DEPARTMENT OF STATE (1948) *Proceedings of the International Civil Aviation Conference, Chicago, Illinois, November 1–December 7, 1944*, 2 vols, Washington, D.C.: US Government Printing Office.

US SENATE (1945) *Convention on International Civil Aviation: Hearings before the Committee on Foreign Relations, United States Senate, February 20–March 26, 1945*, Washington, D.C.: US Government Printing Office.

US SENATE (1946) *International Commercial Aviation*, Committee on Commerce, Senate Document 173.

VAN ZANDT, J.P. (1944) *Civil Aviation and Peace*, Washington, D.C.: Brookings Institution.

WARNER, E. (1945) 'The Chicago Air Conference: Accomplishments and Unfinished Business,' in *Blueprint for World Civilization: The Chicago International Conference of 1944 as Viewed by Four Members of the United States Delegation in Recent Magazine Articles*, Washington, D.C.: Department of State Publication 2348.

WASSENBERGH, H.A. (1970) *Aspects of Air Law and Civil Air Policy in the Seventies*, The Hague: Martinus Nijhoff.

WEISS-WIK, S. (1983) 'Enhancing Negotiators' Successfulness: Self-Help Books and Related Empirical Research,' *Journal of Conflict Resolution* 27: 706–39.

WHEATCROFT, S. (1964) *Air Transport Policy*, London: Michael Joseph.

WHITE HOUSE (1978) *United States Policy for the Conduct of International Air Transportation Negotiations*, Washington, D.C.: US Government Printing Office.

WINHAM, G.R. (1977) 'Negotiation as a Management Process,' *World Politics* 30: 87–114.

WINHAM, G.R. (1979) 'Practitioners' View of International Negotiation,' *World Politics* 32: 111–35.

YOUNG, O.R. (1978) 'Anarchy and Social Choice: Reflections on the International Polity,' *World Politics* 30: 241–63.

YOUNG, O.R. (1982) 'Regime Dynamics: The Rise and Fall of International Regimes,' *International Organization* 36: 277–97.

ZARTMAN, I.W. (1976) 'Introduction,' in I.W. Zartman (ed.) *The 50% Solution*, Garden City, N.Y.: Anchor.

ZARTMAN, I.W. (1978) 'Negotiation as a Joint Decision-Making Process,' in I.W. Zartman (ed.) *The Negotiation Process: Theories and Applications*, Beverly Hills: Sage.

ZARTMAN, I.W. & M.R. BERMAN (1982) *The Practical Negotiator*, New Haven: Yale University Press.

# Index